Palaces of the Night
CANADA'S GRAND THEATRES

Copyright ©1999, John Lindsay

Published by:
Lynx Images Inc.
P.O. Box 5961, Station A
Toronto, Canada M5W 1P4
Web Site: www.lynximages.com

Design: Andrea Gutsche & Janice Carter
Cover Design: Janice Carter
Typesetting and Layout: Heidy Lawrance Associates
Lynx Images Inc. 1st Printing, October 1999

Printed and bound in Canada by Transcontinental Printing Inc., Métrolitho Division

Cover image: The Elgin, Elgin and Winter Garden Theatre Centre
Back cover images: upper & lower—John Lindsay collection; middle—Capitol Theatre, Moncton

Canadian Cataloguing in Publication Data

Lindsay, John C., 1933-
    Palaces of the night: Canada's grand theatres

Includes index.
ISBN 1-894073-17-7

1. Motion picture theatres - Canada - History. I. Title.

NA6846.C3L557 1999   725'.823'0971   C99-931532-3

Palaces of the Night
CANADA'S GRAND THEATRES

by

John Lindsay

Montreal's Allen Palace, the Quebec flagship of this Canadian-owned international movie theatre circuit, was one of Canada's most elaborate vaudeville/movie theatres. The unique decorative windows in the ornate auditorium and the elegant frieze did justice to the name "Palace."

Table of Contents

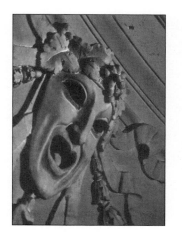

Sincerely—
Mary Pickford.

Foreword

When John Lindsay first asked me to consider writing a foreword to his book about our grand old movie theatres, a flood of marvelous memories came to mind.

What wonderful places they used to be! Those spectacular buildings truly were palaces in the real sense of the word. It is sad that they are nearly all gone now, for they were built at a time when movies were young and they reflected the spirit of our industry.

How well I remember when my pictures were premiered! Most films then were distributed with a musical score meant for a complete orchestra. Only a real movie palace had an orchestra of fifty or more musicians and could handle such a presentation. It always made such a fine start when the conductor proudly bowed, as the spotlights shone down on him as he began the overture. The entire orchestra would rise on a lift and the great audience would burst into applause as the orchestra set the mood for the picture to come. Even the audience was well-dressed and the theatre was nearly always decorated with flowers and banners; and, of course, there were those wonderful kleig lights on opening night with unbelievable crowds of fans in the streets jamming traffic for a glimpse of the stars attending.

The thrill and the glamour of a real premiere, complete with all the show business trimmings only the movie palace could offer, are things we don't experience any more. The silent movie was more effective than a sound one when introduced by a live orchestra, it seemed to lend itself better to the setting of the movie palace.

My husband (Charles "Buddy" Rogers) and I, and our very good friend, Matty Kemp, have spent a good deal of time over the past several years restoring and preserving some of Hollywood's grand old pictures. It is my sincere hope that John Lindsay's beautiful book will help save at least a few of our grand old theatres to show them in, because the movie palace, like those fine old pictures, deserves to be preserved.

Mary Pickford.

The Metropolitan's wide auditorium. The City of Winnipeg has saved this theatre along with the historic Walker Theatre and The Capitol.

Preface

As a young boy in Aylmer, Ontario, my best friend's dad was the projectionist at the Capitol theatre. The theatre had about 200 seats and little or no architectural merit, but it did have fibreglass curtains which changed colours through the use of coloured spotlights and changing foot and border lights. This house curtain opened and closed grandly in front of the small screen before each feature. The screen was mounted on giant rollers so that it, and the sound system behind it, could be moved back to reveal a small stage. Sometimes I was allowed to open the curtains on Saturday afternoons at the top of the movie. "Don't open them too fast," the projectionist would say, "we want it to look like they are opening by an electric motor — just like in the big-city theatres." He was a perfectionist and ran every reel of film through calloused fingers, checking for bad splices so that he would never lose the picture no matter what condition the film was in.

My first visit to a real movie palace—the great Fox Theatre in Detroit—came when I was six years old. I will never forget the performance that evening. The theatre's 6,000 seats were filled with people expectantly awaiting the fantastic stage show to be presented along with the movie. Suddenly, the mighty theatre organ appeared out of the darkness. Then the orchestra magically rose up and slid backwards across the stage before rising again on a huge elevated section of the stage.

When the stage show started, hundreds of dancers swirled around on revolving elevated sections while elaborate scenery seemingly came out of nowhere. The finale was unforgettable. Dancers carrying sparklers paraded down a long staircase and disappeared into a swimming pool in the space from which the orchestra had earlier risen. Needless to say, for me, the Aylmer Capitol was never the same. That evening left a huge impression. I was fascinated not only by the production but also by the theatre itself, and this fascination has led to my lifelong interest in theatre buildings.

Restepping of the Elgin balcony, Toronto, July 1989

I was thrilled when the late Mary Pickford agreed to write the foreword to *Turn Out The Stars Before Leaving*, my first book about Canada's theatres. She appreciated the importance of preserving our movie palaces. When I first started researching Canada's grand theatres twenty-five years ago, I did not realize so many people would share my enthusiasm. Initially, interest in preserving historic theatres appealed to only a few, but as more and more of our theatres were threatened, the number of supporters grew in cities and small towns across the country. It is gratifying to see that the list of Canadian theatres that have been saved from the wrecking ball is growing every year.

Loew's Yonge Street Theatre was a dominant feature on Toronto's Yonge Street c. 1918.

1 THE GRAND & THE NOT SO GRAND

If all the first claims are to be believed, 1896 was a most significant year in movie history. In that year, on April 23, the Holland Brothers of Ottawa presented Edison's Vitascope at Koster and Bial's Music Hall in New York. Canada's Holland Brothers truly were among the great pioneers of the film business. They were entrepreneurs who saw what the movies had to offer. Thomas Edison was so impressed with their ideas that he gave them an exclusive contract to show Edison's films not only in Canada but also in all cities and towns in the United States west of Chicago. It may well have been the Hollands who convinced the great Oscar Hammerstein (whose former Manhattan Opera House was renamed Koster and Bial's Music Hall) to include the first public showing of movies on a screen in a theatre. At the time, Koster and Bial's was one of New York's most successful theatres. The night movies were first shown in Herald Square Koster and Bial's management presented a programme of acts that included William Olschansky, the Russian Clown, Cora Casselli, Eccentric Dancer, and The Three Delevines. These vaudeville turns were followed by film selections such as *Sea Waves*, *Kaiser Wilhelm reviewing his Troops* and *Burlesque Boxing*, all presented on Edison's latest marvel, the Vitascope. These exhausting and thrilling events

In 1896, Canada's motion picture pioneers, the Holland brothers, introduced America to Edison's Vitascope at Koster & Bial's Music Hall in New York. A month or so later they showed movies on a larger screen in their home town of Ottawa.

THIS PROGRAMME is subject to alterations at the discretion of the management.

1 OVERTURE, "Masaniello," Auber

2 WM. OLSCHANSKY
The Russian Clown

3 CORA CASELLI
Eccentric Dancer.

4 THE THREE DELEVINES
In their original act "Satanic Gambols"

5 PAULINETTI and PICO
The Athletic Gymnast and Gymnastic Comedian.

6 MONS. and MME.
DUCREUX-CERALDUC
French Duettists.

7 THE BROTHERS HORN
Assisted by MISS CHARLOTTE HALLETT
"London Life."

THOMAS A. EDISON'S LATEST MARVEL

8 THE VITASCOPE,
Presenting selections from the following:
"Sea Waves," "Umbrella Dance," "The Barber Shop," "Burlesque Boxing," "Monroe Doctrine," "A Boxing Bout," "Venice, showing Gondolas," "Kaiser Wilhelm, reviewing his troops," "Skirt Dance," "Butterfly Dance," "The Bar Room," "Cuba Libre."

INTERMISSION 10 MINUTES
IN THE GRAND PROMENADE
Dr. Leo Sommer's Blue Hungarian Band.
Programme continued on next page.

This programme highlights vaudeville acts and the Vitascope.

Workers Leaving the Factory, Louis Lumière's 1895 film.

were followed by a much-needed ten minute intermission featuring Dr. Leo Summer's Blue Hungarian Band. Such was the stunning bill that night in April when movies became part of a theatre performance for the very first time in America.

A few short months later, the Hollands again presented the Vitascope on an even larger screen in a park in Ottawa. (Many more Canadians had with their first film experience when the Hollands presented *The Great Train Robbery* on the Midway at the Canadian National Exhibition in 1903.)

New research by professors Jean-Marc Larrue (at the University of Quebec in Montreal) and Andre Bourassa (at the Collège de Valleyfield) in their book *Nuits de la Main* (Nights on the Main) claim that the same year in Montreal there was an earlier showing than the one by the Holland brothers:

"...It was in the Hotel Saint Laurent, just beside the Palace (theatre) that Felix Mesguich (a representative of the Lumière brothers in America) presented the Cinematographe Lumière in the month of May 1896. This event took place before an earlier projection in a theatre by a French compatriot, Louis Minier, who showed a series of small films, on the 27th of June, at the Palace, which was the subject of an article in La Presse newspaper the next morning. The hotel no longer exists, but the Palace maintains its distinguished bearing all the same—there are as yet no records to dispute that the Palace was the first cinema in Canada; Mesguich moved on to New York which was to discover the Cinematographe Lumière after Montreal on June 29th..."

It has been reliably reported that Paris saw the very first public performance of the "Cinematograph" (movies) in 1895, and that shows were presented in Lyons, Bordeaux, Brussels and Berlin as well as London. Arguable claims as to which city, entrepreneur, etc. was "first" with the new theatrical device were usually more assertive than was London, Canada's claim. According to that city's *London Free Press*, a feature story in the early part of the century was headlined "LONDON IS ALMOST THE PARENT OF THE MOVIES."

Toronto's "first" was on Aug. 31, 1897 at Robinson's Musee on Yonge Street, where patrons were thrilled with "Professor Roentgen's Great X Rays" (movies). Toronto was so puritanical back then that even the word "vaudeville" was considered vulgar, and unacceptable. Robinson's Musee was about as far from a museum as one could get—offering freak shows, magic lantern shows and movies.

Operated by a Buffalo entrepreneur, Robinson's Musee featured a picture called *The Kiss* and starred Canada's own Mae Irwin from Whitby, Ontario. This now-famous and at the time, shocking short film, also starred John C. Rice. Crowds of people eagerly plunked down ten cents to see the flickering images

Vaudeville developed as a form of cheap and popular entertainment for the working class. A show was comprised of a series of unrelated acts, dancers, singers, acrobats, and animal acts following in rapid succession. Vaudeville was the most important form of entertainment for fifty years, between 1875 and 1925.

The 1896 film Rice-Irwin Kiss *outraged audiences. These first films were little more than unedited clips showing an action or a vaudeville act.*

projected by the Vitascope. The film was dumped into a basket on the floor under the projector and was then collected for the next show.

The idea of showing a few short films with a stage show spread quickly. Also in 1897, a popular opera house manager — the London, Ontario visionary, Al Root — brought the inventor of the cinematograph with his bulky hand-driven apparatus and his troop of performers and interpreters to London, straight from their New York triumph. Londoners, however, failed to applaud the new marvel. The box office receipt for that historic week was a paltry $240.00.

The Black Tent, devised around the turn of the century by Canadian travelling salesman J. Schuberg (alias Johnny Nash), appears to be the only specially designed accommodation for movies until about 1906. Nash's tent measured 20 feet by 60 feet and seated 200 people. Made of black canvas with an interior of black flannel to keep out the sunlight, it had a side wall which could be raised at the end of each show to cool off the patrons. Nash later formed the Nash circuit with small theatres from St. Louis, Missouri to Winnipeg, Manitoba. He claimed to have employed young Al Jolson and Charlie Chaplin in the vaudeville show that accompanied his movie presentations. He showed films such as *The Great Train Robbery* in the Avenue Theatre in St. Louis and on the silver screen in Winnipeg's Unique Theatre (a former funeral parlour).

In Montreal, on January 1, 1906, Ernest Quimet opened his first theatre, the Quimetoscope. The following year he opened another Quimetoscope in the same city. It was a 1,000-seat mini-picture palace (complete with its own seven-piece orchestra) which has legitimate claim to the title of the world's first theatre devoted only to movies. It was here that, for the first time, special prices were set for matinee and evening performances. In 1907 Quimet claimed to have shown the first

Johnny Nash, one of Canada's earliest movie exhibitors

Canadian showman J. Schuberg (alias Johnny Nash) showed movies in a tent at fairs and exhibitions throughout Canada. Sometimes billed as "The Electric Theatre," the Black Tent appears to have been the only specially designed accommodation for movies until about 1906.

The Quimetoscope Theatre in Montreal has the rightful claim as the world's first theatre devoted exclusively to movies.

"sound" movie anywhere by synchronizing a film with his new "French gramophone."

The Quimetoscope was far more elegant and sophisticated than John Griffin's Theatorium which opened in Toronto in 1906. His little theatre was just 17 feet wide and 100 feet deep. Griffin, a former circus showman, thought the term "theatorium" would give the place "class" and distinguish it from the many vaudeville theatres that were then so popular in Toronto. The hand-cranked machine churned out movies from 9 a.m. to 11 p.m. Gus Demery, who successfully answered an advertisement in the newspaper for "an usher at Toronto's first movie theatre," was paid the princely sum of nine dollars per day. As for the other architectural niceties of the Theatorium, 150 cramped patrons paid a

Toronto's first movie theatre, The Theatorium, 1906.

nickel to sit on a plank nailed between two chairs and watch a one-reeler projected onto a bare white wall, lasting a little more than ten minutes. About this same time, Jules and Jay Allen were operating a similar theatrical enterprise in Brantford, Ont.

Movies were still very young in 1906. Little more than a string of peep shows, they were far from the massively popular form of entertainment they would later become. An entire show would last from ten minutes to half an hour and the surroundings were best ignored. Movies were shown in converted stores, penny arcades, dance halls or any other public building (including churches) which could be found on Main Street. Auditoriums were dark—the darker the better—narrow and badly ventilated. Seating often consisted of chairs rented from a funeral parlour.

At a fairly early stage, some movie theatre entrepreneurs realized that the theatre itself could attract business. Many of these small storefront theatres, later

A packed house at Montreal's grand Quimetoscope Theatre

At penny arcades, patrons dropped a penny into a machine then cranked a handle which rapidly flipped a series of photographs printed on cards, giving the appearance of moving pictures. Later movie pioneers like Marcus Loew opened "nickelodeons" above these arcades to show projected moving pictures.

Buildings converted into movie theatres were called nickelodeons. This early nickelodeon in Edmonton seemed more interested in advertising its movies than in impressing customers with a fancy entrance.

called nickelodeons ("nickel" from the cost of admission and "odeon" from the Greek for theatre) had pretenses of grandeur. Some owners would install glass staircases with running water and coloured lights beneath each step. They could purchase an instant theatre front to draw patrons in, a "Coney Island Front," complete with stamped tin stars, sockets for coloured bulbs, and angels with flapping wings. All kinds of statuary, bric-a-brac and fake columns were available to cover the storefront theatre with a stereotypical nickelodeon elegance. Some theatre owners dispensed with the Coney Island fronts altogether and came up with something really unique. One such theatre was the Opera House in Canmore, Alberta which was built entirely of logs. This "little house on the prairie" movie theatre did business right into the 1940s.

The 250-seat Starland Theatre in Montreal was typical of this cosmetic camouflage and others appeared in cities all across Canada and the United States. By 1909 there were 8,000 nickelodeons in the United States, 600 in New York alone. The Starland had a brave, star-spangled front, literally glued on at a cost of nearly two thousand dollars.

If the tin stars, flashing lights or frenetic angels failed to entice one in to see the show, there was always the persuasive, gravel-voiced barker extolling the movie's virtues. Nickelodeons like the Idle Hour in the little town of Aylmer, Ontario had their own ways of increasing business. One boy with a hearty laugh was always let in free because he got everybody going. By 1912, small-time vaudeville theatres were presenting regular showings of movies as part of their programmes. This policy began to threaten the nickelodeon. When the bigger vaudeville shows with their big-time stars also included movies, the nickelodeon was doomed.

In 1903, Thomas Edison's studio, headed by Edwin Porter, filmed its movies in a tin shack called "The Black Maria." This was widely reported to be the first American motion picture studio. Here Porter filmed *The Great Train Robbery*, a 12-minute story complete with movie stunts and thrilling action. One

An early photograph of the Palace Grande in Dawson City, the scene of a benefit for the widows and orphans of the Boer War

The asbestos house curtain in the opera house in Biggar, Saskatchewan, was so full of advertising, there was little room for the traditional painted Venetian scene.

The Bijou Theatre, Edmonton, Alberta. The Bijou's façade is a classic example of nickelodeon elegance. Many such theatre fronts were partly prefabricated and glued on, complete with angels and flashing stars. As movies began to threaten vaudeville around 1910, nickelodeons in the U.S. could not have 300 seats or more without having a costly amusement licence. In their Ticket to Paradise, *John Margolies and Emily Gwathmey state that about 25 nickel theatres existed in 1904 in America, in comparison with eight thousand only six years later. Six hundred of these were in New York City alone.*

scene in particular scared the pants off the viewers: when an outlaw pointed the barrel of his gun straight into the camera and fired, seemingly into the audience's face. Edison had a summer retreat in a little hamlet called Vienna, near Port Burwell, Ontario, on the north shore of Lake Erie. Some of his experiments were reportedly carried out there.

Thomas Edison, who was interested in getting his movies shown in as many places as possible, gathered together almost all of the motion picture patents and formed "the Trust" in 1908.

The Great Train Robbery *(1905). The 12-minute film consisted of 14 shots. Crowds were terrified by the final frame depicting the sheriff shooting at the audience.*

The Trust grew out of the all too important Motion Pictures Patent Company on the East Coast. The Trust was broken up by the courts in about 1912. Edison really set back the creative development of the motion picture because he was mostly interested in the science of the movies, rather than their development as an art form.

The Selig Company made motion picture history when it filmed *The Count of Monte Cristo* in Santa Monica, the first film produced in the West, outside of New York. Edison's real rival as far as the production of movies was concerned, however, was Carl Laemmle, a film distributor from the midwestern United States. He fought the Trust and encouraged William Fox and Adolph Zukor to develop "the star system" of making movies. Movies became longer, had real stories and displayed some good production values thanks to men such as D. W. Griffith who was undoubtedly one of the greatest directors of the silent

When completed, D. W. Griffith's The Birth of a Nation *(1915) was three hours long. It became the first big "Hollywood blockbuster." Variety estimates that it earned $50 million.*

era. Camera and production techniques such as long shots, close ups, and intercutting, were all attributed to Griffith. Soon full-length movies like Griffith's *Birth of a Nation* (1913), the most successful movie of its day, played in large theatres, completely bypassing most nickelodeons.

Despite the fancy façades and potted palms, the early movie theatres were very plain, especially when compared to even the most ordinary vaudeville theatres. The nickelodeon was a cramped, stuffy, uncomfortable and poorly-lit building where people went to while away half an hour. Nobody went there for a big night on the town. Two factors were about to change all that: movies became longer, and more importantly, better; and theatre owners found they were competing with vaudeville for the same audience.

The "silver screen" was the term used to advertise the movies, but the people who worked in the theatres called movies the "picture sheet". The picture sheet was understandably hated by many a disgruntled and perhaps soon-to-be-fired stagehand. It ultimately doomed vaudeville and, for a while, almost every type of live theatre as well. But before that happened, the combination movie/vaudeville palace was born. Its irresistible offering of a movie "on our giant silver screen" plus "live on stage now" led to a world where patrons could lose themselves in an atmosphere of pure escapism, where none grew old, least of all the stars.

The combination theatre had its beginnings in shows like the one brought to London, Ontario by the enterprising Mr. Root. Many travelling shows that appeared in local opera houses across North America were fairly spectacular and fore-shadowed the staging effects used in movie palaces. At least one of these travelling shows featured nearly 2,000 feet of motion pictures, singers, dancers, and glass water fountains on either side of the stage upon which stereopticon (3D) slides were projected. It seemed that no expense was spared in obtaining effects to satisfy an audience. One travelling company, Hale's Tours, thrilled audiences on both sides of the Atlantic by using an abandoned streetcar mounted on rollers and a double moving panorama on either side of the car. By simply increasing the speed at which the panorama flew by, it looked and felt like the streetcar was tearing madly through the countryside when, in fact, only the scenery was moving.

An early attraction board

Movie posters are displayed on the sidewalk in front of the Opera House (right), Prince Rupert, B.C.

The Canmore Opera House, Canmore, Alberta. Instead of a typical nickelodeon façade, this little theatre was not ashamed to show it was built entirely of logs. The theatre kept its "Little House on the Prairie" look well into the 1940s before being designated an historic site and moved to an Alberta park.

People flocked to see the shows and it was a pretty small town that did not have a stage of some kind. The stage was often in the town hall/opera house. Whether or not opera was ever performed at the opera house was unimportant. They were called opera houses because the name lent "class" to the building and to whatever was shown there. The truth is that many of these buildings were makeshift structures which doubled as ballrooms, music rooms or meeting rooms.

Some of the theatres left a lot to be desired. In a 1912 *Variety* magazine article, actor Nick Norton describes one of the more trying episodes at one of Canada's less spectacular theatres in Joggins Mines, New Brunswick,

The Haskell Opera House has an auditorium straddling two countries! The border between Quebec and Vermont passes right through the theatre.

Joggins Mine was another corker. A blinding blizzard gave the company a lot of trouble... about sixteen were carried by cutter to the hotel about a mile and a half. It and another inn could only accommodate about three of the troopers as the rooms were all full. The company went to diverse places for the night. The theatre was over the post office and the scenery had to be taken up the front steps. Every time the electrician used the spotlight the whole town was plunged into darkness. All the mines shut down for the show and the company [a one-night company of Madame Sherry] did some business.

Above: Exterior of Toronto's Massey Hall. Bottom: Interior of Toronto's old Massey Music Hall (later called Massey Hall), 1894. A concert hall with excellent acoustics (2,765 seats) it has presented everything and everybody, from the Great Caruso to wrestling.

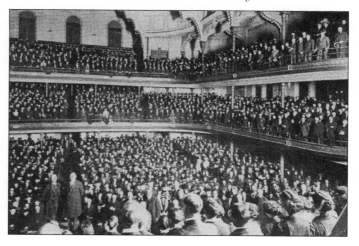

The Victoria Opera House, Victoria, B.C., opened in 1913. It is now called the Royal Theatre.

The lavish interior of Toronto's Grand Opera House. When the theatre first opened on September 23, 1874, an advertisement read, "as an added attraction the Elegant Prismatic Reflecting Sunlight Chandelier will be lighted by electricity every evening at a quarter to eight o'clock."

This all changed around the turn of the century when the Grand Opera Houses of Quebec City, Montreal, Toronto, London and other large Canadian cities began to appear. After the railways had crossed Canada, linking all but the smallest towns, it was possible for theatrical touring companies to move around and to transport their scenery and equipment with relative ease.

Grand Opera House, Toronto

On stage at the Capitol Theatre in Calgary. Full use was made of the rather narrow stage for this spectacular production complete with horses and even airplanes.

Asbestos house curtain for a theatre in Biggar, Saskatchewan. Notice the rather uncomplicated phone number of the A-1 Meat Market.

There were many businessmen who were quick to realize that they could get a good troupe and a good show, even a New York show, if they had a decent theatre. Before long, spurred on by businessmen, every city in the country felt the need to build an opera house. There were profits to be made in luring big companies with popular shows to play in theatres with 1,000 seats or more. The Aylmer (Ontario) Town Hall and Opera House had only 600 seats but even it managed to attract the famous Marks Brother (Ernie Marks) Touring Company from Oshawa, Ontario on a regular basis. St. Thomas, only a few miles away, lured the Marks Company too, but it had three theatres each with about 1,000 seats.

The Minstrel Show was a draw at many "Opera Houses." This one, in Aylmer, often starred local musicians and singers. Aylmer businesspeople supported the productions by buying advertising space on the periphery of the ornate, asbestos fire curtain.

The Aylmer Opera House was built in 1873 but it is not clear when the theatre itself was fashioned out of the enormous meeting room on the second floor. The stage was built out into the main room where the huge palladian windows had to be painted black to keep out the light. A balcony with an elaborate wrought iron railing was added. There was even an enormous Union Jack painted on the ceiling to look like it was waving in the breeze.

The proscenium arch was about 30 by 25 feet and the scenery could be flown out of sight of the audience. The proscenium arch itself appeared to be carved in great detail with columns and pedestals but in fact it was a painted illusion. On either side of the stage were two reassuringly large doors with the word "Exit" painted on them. What was not apparent was that both doors led backstage, with all its ropes, scenery and other paraphernalia, and converged on one very narrow wooden staircase smack in the middle of the rear stage wall!

As the floor was not raked, the sight lines to the stage were not the best. When Guy Lombardo and his orchestra played there, who would have wanted to dance on a slanting floor? The "multicultural auditorium" (multi-use auditorium) which was thought to be so innovative in the 1950s had nothing on the Aylmer Town Hall. Although the place may have been a fire-trap, the knowledge that fire trucks were parked right beneath the theatre must have been some comfort to patrons. The entire building, one of the oldest town halls in the country, has reopened after a wonderful restoration.

The Aylmer Town Hall (Opera House) was built in 1874 in Aylmer, Ontario. Declared an historic site, this building houses one of the oldest theatres in Canada. Its second floor opera house still operates as a theatre.

Poster for the Aylmer Minstrels

The old Opera House, London, Ontario, burned to the ground and was replaced by the Grand Theatre.

The Grand Opera House of London, now the Grand Theatre, was one of the earliest and grandest theatres in the country. This fine theatre ranks with the Grand Opera House, Quebec City (now the Capitol); His Majesty's Theatre, Montreal (razed); the Royal Alexandra, Toronto, and the Opera House, Walkerville (later the Windsor Tivoli). Other theatres of the same vintage and elegance included the Imperial Theatre, Saint John, New Brunswick, and the Walker Theatre in Winnipeg. (The Imperial has been restored as a live venue and the Walker ran for years as the Odeon Morton.)

The Grand in London is the only opera house of its size to run continuously from the turn of the century to the present.

The Grand Theatre (Grand Opera House), London, Ontario, has been operating almost continuously since 1901 making it a real landmark in Canadian theatre.

The original Grand opened in 1880 and occupied the third and fourth floors of the Masonic Temple. It burned down in 1900. The present theatre, which opened in 1901, is still in business. Some smaller opera houses have survived in towns and cities across Canada but none with the performance record of the Grand.

Londoners are always quick to point out that the Grand had the largest stage in Canada, larger than the one at the Royal Alexandra in Toronto. The proscenium arch was the unifying element, with its sounding board, curved to reflect the sound back into the audience. It was painted with gambolling nymphs and was framed on either side by box seats for the wealthier patrons. The less afflu-

The impressive mural over the Grand Theatre's proscenium arch

ent sat in the gods—the second balcony. This balcony was quite large and the seats were raked at an alarming angle so that the audience could see and hear the performers clearly. Even though the balconies were high above the stage, they were not very far back from the footlights. You may have had to spread your knees to peer down to the stage, but you could see the performers and you certainly could hear them.

The Walker Theatre, Winnipeg, Manitoba, c.1907. One of the largest and most important theatres in the West, it was once the hub of an active western theatre circuit. Later, as the Odeon Morton, its top balcony was cut off by a false ceiling. When the false ceiling was removed during renovation, the original artwork was revealed.

The Academy of Music (later the Majestic), opened in Halifax, Nova Scotia in 1877. A fine, legitimate theatre, it had connections to the big-time in the U.S.

The Imperial Theatre in Saint John, N.B. has been wonderfully restored as the province's premiere showcase. Opened in 1913, it had all the elegance and style of contemporary New York theatres. Manager of this grand theatre, Walter Gilding, had a lifelong friendship with Louis B. Mayer who had immigrated to Saint John where he started his climb to the top of the movie world.

The beautiful Tivoli movie theatre of Windsor, Ontario (ex-Walkerville Opera House of Johnny Walker fame). Its grand opera house days are long gone; even its bingo hall days are but a memory.

The Academy of Music (Majestic) in 1913.

Early photograph of a local performance of Dumaurier's big stage hit, Trilby. The stage is unknown but could well be The Academy of Music, Halifax. The woman is Trilby, the bearded actor Svengali, and the violinist, Beppo.

Modern theatre and concert hall designers are always trying to improve the acoustics of old opera house-vaudeville theatres but they seldom succeed. When they do, they often reduce the seating capacity drastically, thus cutting down the viability of the theatre. The new Grand in London, at 800 seats, had only about half of its original seating capacity. Granted, every seat is a good one and that certainly was not true before. Leg room was never considered important in the old theatres, except in the box seats where one could move the chairs as one wished. In common with most Ontario theatres of the time, the Grand had a very drab and rather small lobby. There was no money to be made in the lobby as drinking was forbidden in puritanical Ontario. The lobby bar came into vogue at a much later date.

Detail of painting on the Grand Theatre's proscenium arch

The Grand also had a ghost, which lent the building some intrigue. The ghost was supposedly that of Ambrose J. Small, the one-time owner/manager who later became manager of the Regent Theatre in Toronto and disappeared in mysterious circumstances. The ghost has been sighted on many occasions but it

Letterhead for the Grand Opera House, London. Note the inset of wealthy theatre chain owner, Ambrose J. Small.

The Regent Theatre, Toronto, scene of the famous disappearance of Ambrose J. Small. When Small owned the theatre, it was known as the Grand Opera House.

is hard to say whether or not such sightings were reported because it was good for business. Apparently the ghost has not been seen since the renovation.

It is doubtful if any other opera house in Canada has as successful or interesting a career as the Grand in London, but there were some very early and very interesting theatres right across the country. Built in 1910, Toronto's Shea's Yonge Street theatre was one of Canada's better theatres and was one of the first to bring in hit shows direct from New York. In its 1912-13 showbill, Shea's advertised itself as a first-class building of the finest quality and comfort and the home of good, clean family entertainment,

Attention is called to the fact that Shea's Theatre is Canada's most handsome and modern playhouse. It is constructed of steel, marble and brick throughout. Every appliance and device installed is of undoubted reliability and endorsed and approved by all municipal authorities. The number of exits is largely in excess of official requirement. All exits are plainly marked by lighted signs that may be seen from all parts of the house during all performances at the Theatre.

The theatre is kept scrupulously clean and disinfected by compressed air; the dust that is in and under the carpets, seats

and draperies is drawn from there by compressed air, thus keeping the house clean and sanitary.

Ladies are invited to use the Ladies' Parlours on the Orchestra floor and in the first balcony.

Seats may be reserved by telephone, telegraph or letter, and will be held at the box office until 2 o'clock for the matinee or 8 o'clock for the evening performances.

Patrons who attend Shea's Theatre each week will do well to have their names placed on the subscription. This will ensure them the same seats throughout the season.

Shea's Theatre employees have been engaged on the plane of courteous efficiency. It is the aim of the management to establish an atmosphere of hospitality and congeniality. Complaints of inattention and discourtesy will receive attention.

Physicians who attend the performance will confer a favour on the management by leaving the location of their seats at the box office, as this will facilitate matters in the event of urgent calls.

Spitting on the floor is forbidden by law.

Shea's Yonge Street Theatre. The Shea brothers' first large Toronto house was so successful they soon built the Victoria and the Hippodrome. After the Victoria opened, the Yonge Street theatre changed hands and reverted to burlesque, a raunchy version of vaudeville where audiences were usually male, and smoking was allowed in the seats.

In 1910, Shea's Victoria Theatre, Toronto, was one of the largest vaudeville theatres in North America. Built in grand opera house style with ornate box seats and two enormous balconies it was about a third larger than the Royal Alexandra, built three years earlier.

The Shea brothers built the Shea's Victoria in 1910, a larger 2,000-seat theatre at Richmond and Victoria Streets in Toronto. Soon after this the Yonge Street theatre changed hands and became the Star Burlesque. The burlesque shows, although tame by today's standards, were nonetheless quite vulgar and smoking was allowed in the seats. Although in 1910, Shea's Victoria was Canada's largest theatre, less than three years later, a new Shea's Hippodrome became Canada's largest. Shea's was also affiliated with Keith-Albee, America's most dominant high-class vaudeville circuit. Ontario-born Mike and Jerry Shea became important theatre owners in Buffalo, New York as well as in Toronto. Shea's Buffalo, designed by Rapp and Rapp in the late 1920s, was, and still is, a great American movie palace. This magnificent movie theatre was completely restored and had its stage greatly enlarged in 1999.

Shea's Victoria was a product of Rochester, New York architects L.H. Lempert and Son. The gold-coloured interior was decorated with oak wainscotting and highlighted with gold trimmings. The auditorium's main feature was a mural titled "The triumph of youth." Painted on the sounding board above the proscenium arch, the mural was done by New York City's famous auditorium designers, Harold W. Rambusch Studios. Rambusch Studios went on to become America's foremost movie theatre decorators. Shea's Victoria was a far cry from their masterpiece — the New York Roxy. The 1927 Roxy (6,000 seats) was the world's largest, and many say the most elaborate movie palace ever built.

Some of Canada's grandest vaudeville theatres were built in Toronto, which was one of the big road tour cities between New York and Chicago. Toronto also managed to attract British shows. However, Canadians preferred the American shows and critics sometimes remarked that the audience did not respond to the show because it was "too English." This became a concern at the Toronto Pantages, Canada's largest theatre. Almost all of these theatres showed movies as well as vaudeville but a few did not. These "legitimate" theatres, as they were called, staged plays and musicals, operettas and even

Toronto's Grand Opera House was considered a "legitimate" theatre.

"grand opera." Each of Canada's major cities had at least one legitimate theatre, such as Montreal's His Majesty's and Toronto's Royal Alexandra, which was by far the most famous of all of Canada's legitimate theatres.

The first Yiddish theatre in Toronto was the Lyric, a converted Methodist church. It later became the National, presenting live plays and scenes reflective of the lives of Jewish immigrants. This was not Yiddish Vaudeville. Later, a larger, quite grand theatre was built at Dundas and Spadina streets, first called the Standard and then the Victory. Theatre enthusiast, Izz Gang, recalls an experience he had with his brother at the Lyric. His parents had a dry goods store around the corner and because of the location, they were called on from time to time to lend props. At a very serious moment in the play which was being presented in Yiddish, Izz's younger brother suddenly yelled out from the highest balcony in English: "Izzy, look they are wearing our socks!"

Jerry and Mike Shea were closely connected to The United Booking Office (U.B.O.) of New York, which had a virtual stranglehold on booking "big-time" vaudeville throughout North America in 1913. Shea's Victoria, built in the grand opera house style, with avalanching balconies and

Yiddish vaudeville was featured at the Standard Theatre on Toronto's Spadina Avenue. By the 1940s the theatre had converted to movies and was called the Victory. Later it presented, "Strippers Live On Our Big Stage" and then, after a drastic renovation, it became the "Golden Harvest," showing Chinese movies and occasional live entertainment. It has since been destroyed.

numerous box seats, put Toronto on the map in terms of vaudeville circuits. It later converted to movies and its enormous stage held a big screen until well after World War II. Shea's was fortunate enough to have Canada's most famous vaudeville act, the O'Connor Sisters. They were advertised as the "6 O'Connor Sisters - 6 ✱✱✱✱✱ Vaudeville's only 6 real sisters ✱✱✱✱." These girls were well-respected in big-time vaudeville in the days before the famous Palace was built. They played at Oscar Hammerstein's Victoria Theatre in New York, and later in all the great theatres in America.

According to James Doyle, historian of the O'Connor family, when the O'Connor sisters were starting their careers, critics said of their performance: "although unsophisticated in their stage manner and costume, the blend of the voices won instant acclaim, even the most blasé star rushed to the wings and listened in amazement" (*Early Canadian Life* '78). A Buffalo critic wrote of the girls' first shows: "these girls can sing; in fact their singing has never been surpassed at Shea's. Each girl has a voice of flawless sweetness—they were recalled again and again" (Diary of Ada O'Connor).

The O'Connor home near Toronto, not far from the shores of Lake Ontario, has been in the family since the 1870s and is of historic importance. Here John O'Connor and his wife Joanna had eight

The attractive and multi-talented O'Connor Sisters in an original publicity photograph. Their favourite Canadian theatre was Shea's Hippodrome.

girls and a boy. The older sisters, Anna, Ada, Mary and Nellie, began their stage careers in 1910 and were joined by Kathleen and Vera in 1912. Vera was only 15 years old when she went on stage for the first time at Chicago's Majestic Theatre, then one of the largest theatres in the U.S. When the First World War ended, the O'Connor sisters were offered a three-year tour of Europe. They declined the offer because they did not want to be away from the family for such a long time.

They really were sisters. Madeline O'Connor recalled: "Once we got so tired of people questioning this that our sister Nellie took out an ad in *Variety* saying that 'the O'Connor Sisters are the only 6 real sisters in show business—all others are imposters.'" (The advertisement was aimed at the six

The O'Connor Sisters were the only six ("count' em - 6") real sisters in show business. They were terrific singers. Here they are on stage using a stage set made especially for them.

Kirksmith Sisters, who were not true sisters.) Madeline goes on to say that even her mother had to speak up from time to time to various theatre managers who occasionally bet each other whether the sisters were real or not: "One night when two managers were arguing about them, Momma said, 'They are real all right because they are mine—and I've got two more at home too.'"

Six voices, all with different ranges and trained to develop terrific volume, filled every theatre and soared over the biggest theatre orchestras. "We never used microphones later on either—there was never any need to." The O'Connor sisters headlined the bill in dozens of America's greatest theatres. They got top billing at New York's Strand Theatre and later at the

Shea's Buffalo also loved the O'Connor Sisters. Shea's Buffalo was built much later than the Shea's theatres in Toronto and is a beautifully-restored, grand American movie palace.

5,000-seat Capitol. Mike Shea of Shea's Circuit in Buffalo, auditioned them and sent a rave notice to B.F. Keith in N.Y.C. This meant that they started at the top, rather than working their way up from small-time vaudeville, because Shea and B.F. Keith were in fact branches of the same circuit. The O'Connors played for two weeks at the Shea's Theatre in Buffalo, then Shea's Theatre in Toronto, before going to New York where they made their summer debut at the Brighton Beach Music Hall. They went on to rave notices and later to top billing everywhere. Naturally the girls played Shea's Theatres in Toronto, all three of them. As each new theatre was built, the O'Connor Sisters became part of the show.

Shea's Victoria was totally eclipsed by Shea's Hippodrome (3,200 seats) which opened four years later in 1914 on the site now occupied by Toronto City Hall. The Hippodrome was to Toronto what the Palace was to New York or the Palladium to London. It attracted the very best vaudeville acts from all over the world. Although it was not Canada's most beautiful theatre, it had a great theatre organ and an excellent orchestra.

Red Skelton was one performer whose career took off because of his appearances at Shea's Hippodrome. He stayed in Toronto for a year in 1936 and left a famous entertainer. Grateful, he has been reported at various times as saying: "I really got started in a big way when I went to Shea's in Toronto."

Shea's was the home of big-time vaudeville. The shows arrived direct from the famous B.F. Keith theatres in New York. The difference between big-time vaudeville and two-bit or small-time vaudeville was that the big-time shows had several big name

Little Freddy Mottram, aged five, in 1913. He was one of the youngest singers ever to appear on stage at Shea's Victoria Theatre and his spectacular voice helped to raise money for the war effort.

The ever-popular Ziegfeld Follies was a "big-time" vaudeville show.

stars and quite an extravagant show while the two-bit vaudeville relied on one star surrounded by a number of lesser known performers. Two-bit vaudeville, as the name implies, charged a lower admission price and put on more shows per day.

The Princess and the Royal Alexandra, neither of which presented movies, rivalled the Victoria and Hippodrome. The Princess, which had a reputation for presenting big shows and big stars, operated well into the 1930s. Movies had sound by then and were all-powerful. Movies were the final blow for the Princess, as they were for thousands of other theatres all over the world. Even the great George M. Cohan only attracted an audience of about thirty the last night at the Princess. It was torn down in 1934 to make way for an electrical shop, and for the widening of University Avenue.

These performers from the Ontario Booking Office would have been considered two-bit performers: Jack Paterson, "Canada's favourite Scotch comedian"; Sergeant Kelly, "eccentric comedian"; and Bert Bright, "the black face" who was billed as "everything to amuse, nothing to offend."

The new Princess Theatre in Montreal was much larger and more ornate than Toronto's Princess. The Montreal Princess was the exclusive home of big-time vaudeville in Montreal.

The Princess was a beautiful theatre with an excellent reputation for fine shows. It was the scene of the great early musicals, like "Chu Chin Chow," and was considered to be a high-class house in every respect. It was the Princess which saw a truly significant event—the debut of Mary Pickford, the world's first great movie star. Little Gladys Smith was born on University Avenue on April 8, 1893. As a child actress, she appeared in a play called *The Silver King*, with the lines "Don't speak to her girls, her father killed a man!" Miss Pickford was five years old, but critics thought she had lots of talent even at that age.

The Princess, Montreal had all the necessary New York connections.

This early image of Mary Pickford shows her as a child working in vaudeville.

Featuring vaudeville & photoplays, Montreal's Regent (built 1916) seated over 1,000 people. The interior was a stunning display of gold and ivory, and included wall panels made of imported french silk.

The Royal Alexandra Theatre, Toronto, 1907.

The Royal Alexandra was built in 1907 and is believed by many to be the most beautiful legitimate theatre in North America. That was the intention of Toronto financier, Cawthra Mulock, when he hired John Lyle as architect. Mr. Lyle built the theatre in the beaux arts style and decorated it in French Renaissance. The mural over the proscenium arch and on the sounding board (which is curved plaster to deflect the sound from the orchestra pit to the rear of the orchestra and into both balconies) is 28 feet wide and 12 feet high and depicts Venus and Adonis. It was designed and executed by Frederick Challener, a member of the Royal Canadian Academy of Artists. The beautiful Royal Alexandra remains very popular.

The Royal Alexandra Theatre, owned by "Honest Ed" Mirvish, is considered by some to be the most beautiful "legitimate" theatre in North America.

Royal Alexandra plaster detail

Detail of ornate newel post, Royal Alexandra Theatre, Toronto

The lovely Capitol of Brantford, a large 1,800-seat vaudeville-movie theatre, is one of the few old theatres in Ontario that is still in one piece and not split into a multi-cinema. This theatre was the only big house built by the American movie palace architect Thomas Lamb that was not intended for a big theatre circuit. Rather, it was built for the Allens of Brantford before they had built up their huge Canadian theatre circuit. The Capitol was built as a stadium-type theatre, meaning it had a steeply-raked section at the rear of the orchestra instead of a balcony. For a theatre built before 1920—before the movie palace era—it was

The Temple Theatre (later the Capitol and now the Sanderson Centre for the Performing Arts) was one of the earliest large theatres built for the Allen Circuit of Brantford, Ontario. It is seen here before its restoration.

very large and extremely elaborate. The walls and ceiling were decorated in a Spanish Renaissance style, with a great deal of wrought iron, cut stone, medallions and tapestry.

One visitor to the Capitol, perhaps a little more tactless than most, was A.J. Balaban of the great Balaban and Katz American theatre circuit in Chicago. One day, after admiring the theatre, he turned to the manager and asked, "Why in the hell did they ever build a great big beautiful theatre like this in such a hick town?" The manager kept his cool and mentioned that although Brantford was not the biggest town in the world, the Capitol theatre was not its only claim to fame: Alexander Graham Bell had, after all, invented the telephone there. The Capitol was designated an historic site and continues to operate as The Saunderson Centre for the Performing Arts.

The Lyric and Capitol theatres in Kitchener were two other surprisingly grand theatres built in a small city. The Lyric is especially interesting for its classical statuary on either side of the stage. The Pantages Theatre in Hamilton was another large, beautiful theatre in a relatively small city. It was also designed by Thomas Lamb and bore a strong resemblance to the Loew's London theatre and to the Capitols in Windsor and Winnipeg. All three owed something in their design to the Brantford Capitol.

Brantford's beautifully-restored Capitol was built by Thomas Lamb (1919) and was one of his earliest Canadian creations. The theatre became the prototype of many of Lamb's medium-sized theatres. With 1,500 seats, it was a large and extremely elaborate theatre for a relatively small city.

The Pantages' vertical sign dominated Toronto's Yonge St. in the 1920s.

Alexander Pantages had a large theatre circuit in both the United States and Canada. The Pantages of Hamilton, Winnipeg and Edmonton were all popular, while the Hollywood Pantages, home of the Academy Awards for many years, was the circuit's most famous theatre. The largest was in Toronto and, with 3,626 seats, it was Canada's largest theatre.

When Alexander Pantages was arrested for child molestation, the name Pantages was taken down from every marquee in Canada almost overnight. Not so in the States, however, perhaps because Canada seemed so far away and the crime was not widely reported south of the border. Perhaps a more practical reason was that marquees cost a lot of money!

Northern Ontario also had some very impressive theatres. The Palace in Timmins had a domed ceiling, box seats surrounded by real marble columns (not plasterized, marbleized or otherwise faked as they were in Toronto) and nearly 2,000 seats which were fitted out in luxury. After all, the miners, especially the gold miners, did have money and Toronto was a long way to go for entertainment like this. The thinking behind the Palace

The Palace Theatre in Timmins, northern Ontario, was a first-class house in all respects. Silver leaf used in decoration was made from the real thing.

was the same as that behind the building of the grand movie palaces of the next era: people love to get dressed up and go out some place really special. What better place to go on a cold winter evening than the Palace? Sadly, like other Palaces in Canada, it is now deserted and unheated, a virtual wreck. Several surviving theatres, like the Allen's Palace in Montreal, have been turned into multi-cinemas.

Films such as D.W. Griffith's big spectacle Intolerance (1916) *helped bring on the death of vaudeville.*

In those wonderful years of live vaudeville acts and "select photoplays" (selected screenings), it really didn't matter whether you went to the theatre in the middle of the movie or not. In fact, most people did not even bother to read the movie ads in the paper. They went to see the show and the movie was only part of it. Little by little, movies got longer and better and vaudeville began to slip into second place in the big downtown theatres. By 1918, movies attained a respectable status, about the time that stars like Mary Pickford gained control of their own productions.

Mary Pickford in Little Annie Rooney

Mary Pickford was the one star who nourished the motion picture industry from the nickelodeons to the enormous business it is today. No other performer exerted such influence. She became the first female superstar. The fame she achieved was unequalled by any other woman in her day. Before talkies were invented, when the silent picture transcended language barriers the world over, Mary reigned as the most popular star in the world, and also one of the wealthiest. Before her retirement in the mid-1930s, she had made over 200 films.

Mary had not always believed that films would become the huge success they later did. In 1905, while performing on stage in Chicago, she saw a hand-tinted film from France. The movie, by the Lumière brothers, was only seven minutes long and had caused a sensation when it was shown at Montreal's elegant His Majesty's Theatre a year earlier. Miss Pickford was not very impressed and didn't think the movies would ever rival live stage performances.

Between 1910 and 1920, quality vaudeville slowly gave way to movies, and theatres were constructed at an incredible rate all over North America. There was intense competition among the various movie theatres to lure patrons away from vaudeville and legitimate theatres as well as from each other. Every theatre owner felt that his building must have something different, something more exotic than the vaudeville theatre could offer. It was from this competitive fervour that the escapist architecture of the movie theatre evolved, hand in hand with the escapism of the silver screen.

During this period, many early vaudeville or combination theatres converted to movie theatres. In 1916, Toronto's Grand Opera House was completely redesigned by Thomas Lamb — perhaps the world's foremost movie theatre architect — after it had been sold by Ambrose Small to the Famous Players chain. It re-opened as the Regent and was advertised as Canada's most beautiful theatre. Its white and gold interior boasted an $11,000 Casavant Concert Organ along with a reading room, promenade, and a reception room.

Posters were important marketing tools as movies became big business. This diagram for Buccaneers *was used to show theatre owners different styles of posters and how they were displayed.*

Canadian Theatre Organist, orchestra leader, and broadcaster, Horace Lapp described one horrible experience at the Regent,

> In one show there came a time in the musical performance when an elephant was to rear up on its hind legs and let out a great trumpeting bellow. The elephant's handler was drunk most of the time while he was here, which led to this unforgettable incident. The elephant reared up alright, and trumpeted, but then promptly peed all over the stage! What seemed like tons of yellow stuff poured over the edge of the stage like Niagara Falls, soaking our music stands, clothes and damned near everything else!

The Regent Theatre in Toronto was Famous Players' premiere movie theatre for some years. It was originally the Grand Opera House, the scene of theatre owner Ambrose J. Small's disappearance.

Harold Pfaff, a famous Canadian motion picture pioneer whose long career has spanned a lifetime of motion picture exhibition, recalls the opening night. He stood outside the Regent Theatre watching the festivities from across the street. There he met, and talked briefly with, a most disturbed older man—Ambrose J. Small. Ambrose Small said to Harold, "I'll get it back. I'll get it back. Movies will never make it at the Regent!" That was just about the last time anybody ever saw or heard from Small again.

Years later, when the Regent was torn down, the wrecking crews were asked to search for the remains of Ambrose J. Small because his complete disappearance after the opening of the Regent remains one of Canada's greatest mysteries. Was he murdered by an assassin hired by his wife? Had she found the key to his secret boudoir hidden in the furthest reaches of the Grand Opera House? Had she discovered that Ambrose had a mistress? Was he murdered for the vast sum of money he had made on the sale of his theatre empire? (He sold the theatres for one million dollars on Dec. 2, 1919 and the day his wife

$50,000 REWARD

Missing from his home in this city since December 2nd, 1919

Ambrose J. Small

I am authorized by Mrs. Ambrose J. Small and Capital Trust Corporation to offer a reward of $50,000 for information leading to the discovery of the present whereabouts of the above named man, if alive.

Description: Age 53, 5ft. 6 or 7 ins.; 135 to 140 lbs. Blue eyes, sallow complexion. Brown hair and moustache, streaked with grey. Hair receding on temples. Is very quick in his movements.

Mr. Small, who is well known in theatrical circles in the United States and Canada, was owner of Grand Opera House, Toronto, and was last seen in his office at this theatre on afternoon of December 2nd, 1919.

When last seen he was wearing a dark tweed suit and dark overcoat with velvet collar and a soft felt hat.

The above photo, although taken some time ago is a good likeness, except that for a considerable time previous to his disappearance he had been wearing his moustache clipped short.

I am also authorized to offer in the alternative, a reward of $15,000 for information leading to the discovery of the present whereabouts of the body of the above named man, if dead.

The information must be received before September 1st, 1920, on which date the above offers of rewards will expire.

All previous offers of rewards are withdrawn.

Wire all information to the undersigned.

H. J. GRASETT,
Chief Constable.

POLICE HEADQUARTERS,
TORONTO
June 1st, 1920.

Reward poster for the missing Ambrose J. Small, theatre chain owner, wealthy opera house manager/owner, entrepreneur. Small became one of Canada's most famous missing persons.

deposited the cheque he withdrew the cash and disappeared.) Did he start a new life somewhere else under a new identity? Why did he have a second, smaller, bulletproof office?

Small's first purchase had been Toronto's Grand Opera House. He later took over some 62 Ontario theatres. Along the way, he most assuredly made some enemies. According to entertainment reporter, Mitch Potter, in *The Toronto Star* on June 6, 1999,

> *New York casino operator John Fisher, reportedly once travelled from Manhattan to Toronto for the singular purpose of reaming out the wily Small. But Fisher was mistakenly directed to the office of Small's arch rival, Princess Theatre owner O.B. Sheppard. "Ambrose J. Small, I am the man you swindled," shouted Fisher. "I have never seen you before, but I wanted you to know I have come all the way to Toronto to tell you that you are a damned thief and a liar." Sheppard is said to have answered: "I am glad to meet you Mr. Fisher. It could be that I am a damned thief. I might even be a damned liar. But you cruelly insult me, sir, when you call me Ambrose J. Small."*

To this day, nobody knows what happened to theatre mogul Ambrose Small. Despite Small's prediction, movies certainly did make it at the Regent. They made it so big, in fact, that Famous Players bought or built hundreds more theatres.

Although movies were steadily improving, a good stage show was still necessary for a successful movie theatre. Jack Arthur's shows at the Regent were among the best. Arthur produced excellent reviews with big casts, fine musicians and great dancers. He really was responsible for putting Canadian shows on the theatrical map.

As a child in Scotland, Jack Arthur was an exceptionally talented violinist. By the time he came to Toronto with his father in 1906, he was an experienced member of a troupe of performers supporting the famous Sir Harry Lauder. Apparently his first big job was that of musical director at the Loew's Winter Garden in Toronto. Later he introduced a full orchestra to accompany films at the Regent and made it a memorable event by arranging his own music to match the mood of the pictures. In the days before silent movies included suggested music to accompany them, Jack Arthur wrote original scores for each movie, often once a week. His blend of classical music, tab-opera (opera excerpts), ballet and popular tunes, involving both chorus and high-kicking chorus-girls put him in great demand. Later he went on to much bigger stages and theatres like Shea's Hippodrome, Loew's Uptown and the Imperial.

This advertisement shows how important Jack Arthur was as a Toronto showman. The Imperial was part of the great Paramount—Publix Circuit which sent shows to first run big-city theatres throughout North America.

According to Potter's *Toronto Star* article,

> *...Arthur's reputation was galvanized in 1924 when he surprised and delighted Toronto by declining a generous offer from famed newspaper magnate William Randolph Hearst to work his considerable magic with Hearst's stateside theatre chain. 'Canada has been good to me,' Arthur explained when word had leaked of his passing over the $30,000 contract, thus becoming Canada's first stay-at-home impresario. In the next few years, a generation of Toronto musicians and producers would sprout from Jack Arthur's orchestra.*

Years later when live shows, orchestras and organists were no longer featured in movie palaces, Arthur took an executive desk job at Famous Players. This was certainly not the end of his career as a showman. His 17-year stint staging grandstand spectaculars for Toronto's Canadian National Exhibition was to follow. These shows may have seemed corny to the critics but audiences loved them. Each year he tried to make them bigger and more spectacular. The stage was twice the size of the one at Radio City Music Hall, and could hold a cast of about 400. The headliners arrived in all sorts of theatrical ways: by helicopter, as part of a huge military-style parade, on a fire truck, even on an elephant. Each show featured the world's longest chorus line, The Canadettes, and ended with a grand display of fireworks. The shows, which ran for two weeks, featured such stars as Bob Hope, Danny Kaye and Phil Silvers. The shows attracted bigger audiences than any of Toronto's theatres, and even Radio City Music Hall. Jack Arthur lived to be 81 and died in 1971.

One of the first big theatres designed in Canada especially for the movies was the Tivoli. "Canada's House of Hits" was built in a big stadium-style with what appeared to be a gigantic balcony sweeping down almost from the ceiling to the orchestra floor. Designed by C. Howard Crane and opened as the Allen, the Tivoli boasted a very wide stage and Toronto's brightest and biggest screen. The theatre's policy for awhile was to show movies accompanied by a symphony orchestra on a reserved seat basis.

Luigi Romanelli was the orchestra's flamboyant conductor. (His real name sounded much less impressive.) He was a skilled and hard-working musician who often wrote his own scores for special movie presentations. One night, as Luigi bowed at the end of his overture to the film, his tuxedo tails caught in the Tivoli's rising house curtain, yanking him several feet in the air before dropping him unceremoniously on the floor.

The Allen Theatre, Toronto, later the Tivoli, was one of the first big theatres to be designed especially for movies. It was built in a huge stadium-style with what appeared to be a huge balcony that swept down almost from the ceiling to the orchestra floor. (Today, stadium-style movie theatres are being advertised as the latest innovation in state-of-the-art megaplexes.)

Marion Hanna was introduced to Toronto theatres as an usherette at the Tivoli. She tells what it was like to work there in its early days:

> We all wore cute uniforms with long velvet pants and a jacket which looked like a little tuxedo.
>
> The white gloves we wore had to be spotless, we used the gloves a lot to give hand signals to each other. We always worked in pairs of boys and girls. If one of the girls needed some help in dealing with a difficult male patron, a quick flick of the wrist with the white glove sent a male usher to her right away. Sometimes the boys would signal us too, if they felt a female usher was perhaps better coping with other situations. We had quite a few hand signals.
>
> Once a year around Christmas time the Tivoli would put on a spectacular pantomime. The usherettes and some of the ushers would be selected to appear on stage to augment the New York cast. We were rehearsed for about a month by Leon Leonidoff and his assistant Florence Rogge. He was a wonderful choreographer, and they were both terrific teachers. Mr. Leonidoff went on to the Roxy and then to the great Radio City Music Hall after doing shows in several other Toronto theatres. Luigi Romanelli and his brother were very nice people to work for too. I remember once when we were doing Peter Pan the headliner from New York suddenly flew off the stage and fell into the orchestra pit breaking her ankle. A Toronto gal replaced her immediately for the rest of the show, until they brought somebody else from New York.

To standardize hand signals used by ushers, this card was used for training theatre personnel.

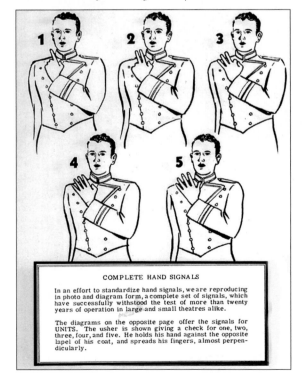

COMPLETE HAND SIGNALS

In an effort to standardize hand signals, we are reproducing in photo and diagram form, a complete set of signals, which have successfully withstood the test of more than twenty years of operation in large and small theatres alike.

The diagrams on the opposite page offer the signals for UNITS. The usher is shown giving a check for one, two, three, four, and five. He holds his hand against the opposite lapel of his coat, and spreads his fingers, almost perpendicularly.

The Allen Theatre as it appeared when it opened. "Canada's House of Hits" was designed by C. Howard Crane.

The Tivoli did great business into the 1950s, but later struggled with wide screen presentations for many years. The Tivoli was the first theatre in Toronto to use the new Todd A.O. process which was shown on superwide screens. For awhile it did quite well with hard ticket sales (premium prices paid in advance for reserved seats) and special blockbuster movies, but by the 1970s, it was finished. The Tivoli disappeared without so much as a single protest.

Although the Tivoli was the Allen Theatre circuit's premiere showcase in Toronto, and was Canada's largest purpose-built movie theatre at the time, it soon found difficulty competing

Luigi Romanelli, the Tivoli's flamboyant conductor

The Allen (Tivoli) was the flagship of the Allen's several Toronto theatres. (The Allen Danforth, later called the Century, is still offering movies and even the occasional stage show. Its current moniker is "The Music Hall.")

with "combination" theatres. These theatres, like Shea's Hippodrome and the Pantages, showed first run movies but offered spectacular stage shows too.

By the end of the First World War, the time was right to build big theatres with thousands of seats, to offer spectacular stage shows with a cast of hundreds on revolving, elevated stages with rising orchestras and spiraling Wurlitzers. As everyone was falling in love with movies, it was time to build a proper showplace for them. Theatre owners wanted to dazzle their customers with both the show and the building. And if they could sell up to 30,000 tickets for one theatre in a single day, all the better.

The Palace Theatre, Englehart, Ontario. Many small-town theatres were far from grand but they still adopted names that implied they were.

The Empress in Fort McLeod, Alberta has a neon tulip on the ceiling.

The Eden Theatre in Sorel, Quebec, featuring The Last of the Mohicans.

Regal Theatre, Rouyn, Quebec, a small-town theatre that drew big crowds.

The Royal Alexandra Theatre, Toronto has an unadorned fire curtain while most safety curtains of the period displayed colourful painted Venetian scenes. These asbestos curtains fitted so tightly to the walls of the proscenium arch that smoke and flame could not creep around them. For years the law stated that the asbestos curtain had to be lowered and raised in front of the audience. It was very reassuring to see "FOR THINE ESPECIAL SAFETY" printed in big bold letters across some asbestos curtains.

As early film for movies was made of highly flammable acetate, it would burst into flames if a film jammed in the projector in front of the white-hot carbon arc light. The projectionist had only a short few seconds to trip the wire holding up the steel plates over the windows as he fled for his life. One or two reels would go up in flames producing noxious fumes which were sucked up ventilator shafts (visible in photo). This system worked so well that few lives were ever lost through fire in a projection booth. There were many cases when the audience remained stamping their feet and clapping, demanding the film be restarted, when in fact the projectionist was seriously burned.

WEATHER FORECAST
Fresh to strong northerly winds; partly cloudy and colder, with light local snowfalls.
For complete weather report see page seven.

The G

VOL. CLVI. No. 8   **LATE EDITION**   MONTREAL, MONDAY, JAN

**SEVENTY-SIX CHILDREN KILLED IN
IN EAST ST. CATHERINE STREE**

**JAM OCCURRED
ONLY 5 STEPS
FROM SAFETY**

Law Prohibits
Unguarded Minors
Being Admitted

**TWO FAMILIES
BEREAVED BY
LOSS OF THREE**

74 VICTI
AT T

The Empress Theatre in Moncton, New Brunswick, burned during a March night. Note the smoke escaping from the stagehouse at the rear of the building. If a fire occurred during a performance, this area was sealed off from the rest of the building by closing dressing room doors and dropping an asbestos curtain. This turned the stage area into a giant chimney which sucked smoke and flame away from the audience.

The blackened interior of the Laurier Palace after the tragedy that killed 76 children. The fire started from a discarded cigarette in the balcony that produced considerable smoke. The children fled down a cement staircase which led directly to the street but the exit door could not be opened. In the stampede to escape many were trampled to death. The theatre was relatively new with all its built-in safety features working at the time of the disaster, but building safety codes cannot preclude criminal negligence.

ette.

TEMPERATURE YESTERDAY
Max., 13; Min., 4

SAME DAY LAST YEAR
Max., 28; Min., 8

927.—TWENTY-TWO PAGES

PRICE FIVE CENTS

C ON STAIRWAY AT FIRE
VIE THEATRE SUNDAY AFTERNOON

NTIFIED
GUE

FOUR MEN HELD
FOR INQUEST ON
PANIC VICTIMS

LANE ATTACKS BRIDGE
Becoming Real Evil Among
Women Players
Special Cable to the N.Y. Times and
Montreal Gazette.
London, January 9.—Sir William

CLARITY OVER
OCEAN 'PHONE
WAS AMAZING

Detail of the Runnymede Theatre. Images projected on walls and ceilings created the hallmark effect of the atmospheric theatre.

2 THE ATMOSPHERICS

It was the goal of the movie palace architect to transform worlds, to transport patrons from their ordinary surroundings to something different, something exotic and palatial. While the atmospheric theatre achieved this even when a theatre was very small, the glamorous "hard top" movie palace, with its domed ceiling, box seats and gold leaf, worked best on a large scale.

Neither of these styles would impress the artistic elite. They were bastardized architecture, wherein many styles were mixed to create a marvelous orgy of architectural excess. Italian Renaissance, Robert Adam, even Persian architecture were superimposed indiscriminately on each other, with little or no regard for historical authenticity. The Empress Theatre, Montreal was typical of this style. In the 1920s, patrons were transported into a Pharoah's paradise upon entering The Empress. Its design was in keeping with the Egyptian craze in theatre decoration and architecture which became popular after the discovery of King Tut's tomb in the 20s. The Empress was the only Egyptian-styled atmospheric built in Canada, all to please the movie patron. Moviegoers might have arrived on a streetcar and paid only 15 cents admission, but when they stepped off that streetcar they knew they had arrived somewhere special! They may not have studied art or visited the

Egyptian heads and scarabs featured prominently in The Empress Theatre, Montreal.

The great popularity of silent film star Rudolph Valentino in The Sheik *made the Empress' Egyptian decor even more stylish and popular.*

Front hall, the Empress

capitals of the world, but they could not help but be impressed by the building's grandeur. The bigger the building, the higher the ceiling, the more flamboyant the decoration, the more they loved it.

In his excellent book about American movie palaces, *The Best Remaining Seats* (Bramhall House, New York, 1961), Ben Hall describes the atmospheric movie palace as "an acre of seats in a garden of dreams" and "cloudland created." The idea really went back to the various Winter Gardens of the British legitimate theatre. Theatre in a garden setting was certainly not new, but North American ingenuity made it something fantastic.

In the tacky, phony, crazy, wonderful world of theatre make-believe, atmospheric movie palaces were the ultimate; they were larger than life. The key to their success was that they were exotic and fascinating, yet cost very little. Ceilings which appeared to be open to the sky were really just ordinary plaster painted a very light blue on which moving clouds, stars, moons and even birds and aeroplanes were projected. In some theatres,

The magnificent view from the Empress' balcony

the moon rose on the left-hand side of the proscenium arch and over the course of the evening's performance moved across the sky, waning over the box seats on the right-hand side of the stage. The atmospherics might have increased the illusion by transforming the side walls of the theatre into the walls of an Italian villa over which one could see the tops of real trees. Real fountains might have tinkled in a niche on a side aisle and forced air might have blown a summer breeze.

The lounge at the Empress in Montreal

This architecture enthralled people for many years. The atmospheric effects were easily produced with a $290 purchase of the Brenograph Junior projector. This made the atmospheric far cheaper than the crystal chandeliers, marble statuary, stained glass, domes and gilt that adorned the hard-top movie palaces. And the effect was just as eye-popping, if not as tasteful. At the

While Cornwall's Capitol and the Runnymede in Toronto were smaller than American atmospherics, they offered the same form of escapism. The Capitol in Cornwall has been razed.

Runnymede Theatre, Toronto, a backstage sign on the lighting panel read "TURN OUT STARS AND SHUT OFF THE CLOUDS BEFORE LEAVING." This was not some kind of celestial instruction; it was a reminder to staff not to let the clouds on the ceiling drift by needlessly all night. This sign might just as well have been posted in the Capitol Theatre in Cornwall, Ontario or the Grenada in Sherbrooke, Quebec. Dozens of theatres in many parts of the world had similar warnings.

Although it was not a true atmospheric, the Winter Garden in Toronto can be classed as the forerunner of the North American atmospheric movie palace. It was built in 1914, about five years before the height of the movie palace era. It dazzled everybody in 1914 and had the same effect when it re-opened in the 1980s. In fact, it is all the more impressive today because few atmospheric theatres remain.

Built in 1927, the Runnymede was the first atmospheric built in Canada. It has now been thoughtfully renovated and serves as a spectacular Chapters Book Store.

Clouds and stars were projected over the proscenium arch at the Capitol in Cornwall, Ontario. The barrel-vaulted ceiling of azure blue completed the scene. The Capitol and the Runnymede were near twins.

Runnymede Theatre, Toronto, c.1927

The Loew's Winter Garden survived intact having been virtually sealed off since 1928. In that year, a decision was made not to install sound but to close the theatre and wait to see what developed. What a long wait she had! The 1928 decision likely saved the Winter Garden from renovations which would surely have ruined her. Instead, she has watched her sisters, like the Princess and the Shea's theatres, have their moments of glory, then disappear. Now it is her turn to bask in a little glory.

Loew's Winter Garden perches seven stories above the street and piggybacks the 2,194 seat Loew's Vaudeville Theatre, currently the Elgin. Both theatres were designed by Thomas W. Lamb, who later became one of the world's foremost movie palace architects. Lamb worked in association with Stanley Makepeace of Toronto. Construction began in 1912. The lower theatre opened December 15, 1913 and the Winter Garden, which seated 1,422, opened February 17, 1914. The

The Winter Garden stage. Its ceiling is covered with wisteria blossoms, rosebuds and silk oak leaves. Photo taken before restoration.

total cost was $1.4 million. That price tag made it one of the most expensive theatres ever built, and it was touted in certain advertisements as the "most expensive playhouse in the world." It wasn't, but neither was it cheap. (One of the problems faced by theatre historians is the fact that nobody in show business ever builds just a theatre, they build the world's best, biggest, most expensive, most beautiful theatre with the greatest shows and biggest acts ever seen anywhere!)

The Winter Garden moon peeks through tree branches which frame the stage and reach up into the painted plaster sky on the sounding board.

Thomas Lamb was just becoming successful as a theatre architect when he designed this theatre and two others long gone, in the United States. The Winter Garden is one of the most unusual theatres anywhere in the world. Instead of having the usual classical columns on either side of the stage, the Winter Garden has tree trunks which branch out and cross over the proscenium arch. Above all of this is a sounding board, a curved plaster shell, on which a blue sky is painted complete with mountains, fluffy clouds and tiny stars.

The Winter Garden's ceiling consists of thousands of real fireproof leaves cleverly woven on branches and lattices and hung by hidden wires attached to real beech branches. Even the pillars of the balcony and box seats are made to resemble tree trunks. Three-dimensional branches subtly fade into two-dimensional painted ones. The three boxes on either side of the stage are festooned with flowers. A moon dramatically lights up one side of the prosce-nium arch (it was in eclipse for years as the theatre lay dark.) Wisteria blossoms, rosebuds and silk oak

Oriental curtain at the Winter Garden as seen on opening night, February 16, 1914.

leaves hang everywhere. The walls, stairways and passages are painted with vivid flowers, shrubs, animals and birds. At one time there was even a summer breeze courtesy of hidden oscillating fans.

When the Loew's Theatre opened on December 15, 1913, Marcus Loew and a group of celebrities from New York, including Abe Erlanger, Joseph M. Schenck, Thomas Lamb and Irving Berlin, arrived to celebrate this beautiful theatre which featured "quality vaudeville and select photoplays." On this great

The Winter Garden as it appeared in 1914.

Auditorium of the
Winter Garden

Hemp ropes were a part of the backstage apparatus at the Winter Garden.

The projector in Loew's Winter Garden sat silent from 1928, the year the theatre closed its doors.

occasion, Irving Berlin introduced a new song and Webber and Fields made a courtesy appearance. Loew's Theatre and the new Winter Garden, when it opened a little later, received rave notices from the Toronto critics and patrons alike.

This two-theatre complex was ahead of its time in many ways. Today theatres with more than one auditorium are highly desirable. Marcus Loew wanted the maximum number of people to see his shows. In the days before microphones, a theatre could only be so large; building two theatres under the same roof was the best way to have twice as many people see the same show. Why was it important that they be under one roof? That way Loew only had to pay the actors for one theatre, even though they were performing in two. Performers had to work double time. While the movie was playing downstairs, the vaudeville show played upstairs, and vice versa. This ensured an almost continuous vaudeville and movie offering, a most exhausting grind for the vaudeville performers.

The two theatres represented a marvelous feat of engineering for 1912. It has been reported that over one hundred horses were needed to lift the enormous main beam into place in the lower theatre. It bore the weight of the balcony in the lower theatre and the entire weight of the Winter Garden above.

Before the wonderful rebirth of Loew's Winter Garden, this "ghost theatre" on Toronto's Yonge Street had been silent for 50 years! A walk through it before the renovation was like a trip in a time-machine. Except for missing seats, this fantastic place looked just as it did when its gas-lit stage sprang to life so

The lovely house curtain in Loew's Theatre, Toronto was hand-painted by the New York scenic artist, A. Howard. Hundreds of sequins give extra brilliance.

many years ago. Backstage, the backdrops dating from 1903 were still in place. Hemp ropes, sand bags, light battens above the stage, all were in good condition, waiting to work their magic once again. Seven floors of dressing rooms, none of them comfortable, serviced the two theatres. A freight elevator, large enough to carry an elephant to the Winter Garden, sat silently off stage. Among the wonderful discoveries was a hand-painted, house curtain illustrated by New York scenic designer, A. Howard. Its brilliant Art Nouveau butterflies and sequins were remarkably bright and colourful. The grand staircase, with the great sweeping curve of the marbleized bannister railing, was impressive, even in its rather decayed condition.

In 1928, a fire in the Loew's Theatre orchestra pit and under the stage caused $30,000 damage and was serious enough to close the lower theatre for months. According to newspaper reports, fire fighters found a wall of flames six feet high but, because the asbestos fire curtain was lowered and the sprinkler system worked, the fire was extinguished. There was no structural damage, in spite of the fact that the fire broke out in the middle of the night. The Winter Garden upstairs carried on during repairs.

The lighted marquee of the Loew's and Loew's Winter Garden Theatres, Toronto, beckons, c. 1930.

There were only three elevators to take patrons to the Winter Garden (and for years one of them was filled with popcorn) but these were sufficient. In 1913, vaudeville shows consisted of eight rotating acts. Nobody cared whether they had come into the theatre at some time other than the first act, one simply stayed until the acts were repeated. As for the movies, they were so short and unimportant, at least in terms of story line, that missing parts made no difference.

Loew's presented two-bit vaudeville, that is at least four shows a day with no advance tickets necessary. Usually there was only one big act or star; the rest of the bill was filled by lesser known entertainers. On opening night, Webber and Fields headlined and they were certainly stars, but who ever heard of Miss Sadie Ott? When Loew's opened its new

Uptown (3,000 seats) on Yonge St. near Bloor in 1920, they had three theatres to fill with customers and with shows. The total seating capacity was over 6,000 and they found it almost impossible to find enough good entertainers to fill all three theatres all year. Canadian theatre historian, Gerald Lenton, feels the main reason that vaudeville died was that there were simply not enough great entertainers to supply the 4,000 theatres in North America with one good star every night. There were hundreds of great vaudeville performers, but not 4,000 and no matter how elegant and beautiful the theatre was, if it didn't have a good show, people didn't come.

Two views of the grand lobby of Loew's Yonge Street designed by Thomas Lamb.

Loew's Yonge Street in downtown Toronto was one of the largest and most expensive theatres designed by Thomas Lamb prior to 1915.

Loew's Yonge Street has been beautifully restored and renamed the Elgin.

The Saskatoon Capitol. Built in 1929 it featured a Spanish interior and was the first atmospheric built on the Prairies.

It is likely that the Winter Garden failed partly because performers were unhappy about having to play twice as many shows for one fee. The Winter Garden tried to vary its programme many times but nothing seemed to help it make money. Beautiful and nearly forgotten, the Winter Garden slept away half a century. Its brass-and-velvet-trimmed box seats saw little change, just layers of dust and the occasional visitor. Before its rebirth, "we even celebrated the 50th anniversary of the Winter Garden's closing," says David Dymond, one-time assistant manager. "Naturally nobody was there." (Loew's theatre downstairs was renamed the Yonge and ran until 1982. It was redecorated in 1978 by Famous Players who tried to restore the grand entrance along its former classical lines. Since then, the original Loew's has been renamed the Elgin, and both it and the Winter Garden have been declared historic sites and restored to their original turn-of-the-century elegance.)

The forerunner of the Winter Garden was New York's American Roof Garden above the American Music Hall (earlier called The American Theatre, 1893). In 1908, Thomas Lamb rebuilt the old rooftop venue with a two-storey theatre complete with balcony, boxes and 1,400 seats. According to *Lost Broadway Theatres*, by Nicholas Van Hoogstraten (Princeton Architectural Press 1991) "the new roof theatre had an 'Adirondack Lodge' atmosphere created by false tree trunks and leafy foliage decorations." In fact it was a near twin of the Toronto Winter Garden.

New York's Casino Theatre (1882) was the very first theatre to have shows on its roof, the creative idea of Rudolf

With a plastered and painted "blue sky" ceiling and a façade of a quaint villa, the Saskatoon Capitol was advertised as "a place of splendour created in warm sunny Spain."

Aronson, who was inspired by the pleasure gardens of England. But Aronson had to wait until buildings were more fireproof and the elevator had been perfected before he could transplant gardens to the roof of his New York showplace. In *Lost Broadway Theatres*, Van Hoogstraten says the theatre was too far uptown to be an initial success: "The project was known as Aronson's folly in spite of being backed by the likes of the Morgans, Tiffanys, Goulds, Vanderbilts, and Roosevelts." Yet after this faltering start it was quite successful for a dozen years.

By far the most famous of the theatres with a rooftop auditorium was, and still is, the New Amsterdam, in New York. This theatre has finally been restored after a struggle for survival which was every bit as difficult as the one to save Toronto's Winter Garden. The New Amsterdam was one of the very few theatre buildings to reflect the creative style of the period in which it was constructed. Van Hoogstraten adds: "the New Amsterdam theatre brought Art Nouveau to Broadway with spectacular suc-

The Capitol Theatres in Regina and Saskatoon, Saskatchewan were lovely atmospherics, similar to the Sherbrooke Granada, but built on a smaller scale.

cess... vines and flowers were the primary motifs of the lobbies as well as the auditorium and the promenades behind it."

According to Van Hoogstraten, the only

other theatre to illustrate the contemporary style was the Earl Carroll Theatre (1931), an Art Deco beauty. Apparently, New York's two Radio City Theatres, the RKO Roxy (later The Center Theatre) and the great Radio City Music Hall, both Art Deco and reflective of the style of the times, were not considered "legitimate" theatres. The New Amsterdam was world famous for being the home of the Ziegfeld Follies (1913-27). They were so popular that Ziegfeld put on a second show, "The Midnight Frolics," on the top of the theatre. Stars like Eddie Cantor packed the place after the regular follies had finished. The roof theatre was later named the Danse de Follies, the Dresden, and lastly, the Frolic before becoming a radio studio and rehearsal hall.

One of the earliest and still the grandest of the atmospheric movie palaces was the San Antonio Majestic. It was built by John Eberson, the father of the atmospheric movie palace. Eberson wanted to build something different to capture the imagination of Texans. He realized that a cool spot—perhaps on the rooftop of a theatre which was open to the cool evening sky—would appeal to people who had suffered through a hot Texas day. A design similar to Toronto's Winter Garden would have worked but Eberson felt that a plain sky with a few clouds drifting by would be cheaper, easier to produce and psychologically cooler than a trellis of leaves overhead.

Eberson's San Antonio Majestic was one of the biggest and grandest ever built. It held about 4,200 people, if all the boxes and "Jim Crow" balconies were used. When this theatre was built, black patrons had to use a separate, rear entrance and sit high in the rafters where both the sight lines and sound were

unsatisfactory. (At this time, theatres in the Southern United States without such balconies or other segregated areas did not admit black patrons at all.) The Majestic took two years to build and opened with *All Quiet on the Western Front*. This 1929 premiere was the most spectacular and celebrity-filled that Texans would ever see.

The Majestic Theatre of San Antonio, Texas, was the epitome of the atmospheric movie palace. Built in 1929, it transported patrons to an exotic garden in Spain, under a cool evening sky. It was John Eberson's final atmospheric.

Both the San Antonio Majestic and the Houston Majestic created "cloudlands" which made the audience believe that they were seeing movies "beneath nocturnal skies." The side walls resembled those of Spanish castles, with turrets, elaborate balconies and columns, hanging plants and windows through which the azure sky could be seen. Over the highest walls rose tall, pine trees with stuffed doves to complement the projected doves and clouds drifting across the barrel-vaulted night sky.

The Granada Theatre in Sherbrooke, Quebec, built seven years later, bore a remarkable resemblance to Eberson's Majestic design. The Granada was smaller but the feeling was still there. The same was true of the lovely old Capitols in Saskatoon and Regina.

John Eberson, the foremost exponent of the atmospheric movie theatre, designed nearly 100 of them before the end of the Golden Age of the movie palace. He had begun his prolific career with the Hobitzelle theatre circuit in Texas in 1922 and turned around conventional movie theatre design when he built the Houston Majestic with its plain, curved, plaster ceiling. Variations of the theatre were built all over the world, many by Eberson, and by those who were inspired by his ideas.

Eberson owned Michelangelo's Studio which produced the plaster casting and stock models of arches, trellises, columns and other decorative details which appeared in different theatres throughout the world. In the Paradise Theatre in the Bronx, Eberson had a larger-then-life sculpture of Lorenzo de Medici peering down on the stage show. Other figures from the Italian Renaissance were either sculpted on the proscenium arch or

The Sherbrooke Granada, Canada's most beautiful atmospheric movie theatre

The Granada's fantasy atmosphere even extends into the lobby where a fountain in the shape of a stone boat appears to have just pierced through the wall.

The Sherbrooke Granada bore a remarkable resemblance to Eberson's Majestic Theatre. The side walls resembled Spanish castles, with turrets, balconies and columns, hanging plants and windows through which an azure sky could be seen. Tree-tops pierced the sky above the elaborate walls while projected clouds and stars drifted slowly by.

The ticket seller often sat in a kind of gilded cage or other exotic enclosure.

The Capitol Theatre in Halifax, Nova Scotia, was an atmospheric with a twist. The lobby was atmospheric with clouds on the ceiling, but after crossing a drawbridge from the lobby to the auditorium, patrons found themselves in a giant baronial hall.

over the box seats, or painted on the asbestos curtain. The lobby, as well, was resplendent with painting and sculpture. On the ceiling, a goddess seemed to be floating in space, her arms and legs entwined in movie film. It was an effort to elevate moviegoing to a cultural experience. Alas, the Paradise in the Bronx, although not lost, has been halved into Paradise One and Two!

The grandest of all the American atmospherics is the fabulous 5000-seat Fox of Atlanta, built in 1929. Marye, Alger and Vinour were the architects of this incredible Moorish palace with minarets overlooking Peachtree Street. The Fox is one of very few theatres in the United States to be declared an official National Historic Landmark; the Paramount in Oakland, California and the Ohio in Columbus, Ohio, are others.

The atmospheric movie theatres of the "dirty thirties" fit into the escapist philosophy spawned by the Depression. In Halifax, Nova Scotia, the Capitol boldly opened its doors in the fateful year of 1929. It was a fascinating building and offered a unique variation on the atmospheric theatre. It had an atmospheric lobby complete with clouds and stars, but once patrons crossed over a drawbridge, they entered the non-atmospheric theatre auditorium which looked like an enormous baronial hall, even to its timbered ceiling and mural of the fortress of Louisbourg. Many servicemen had a warm spot in their hearts for this theatre as it was here that many had spent their last night before being sent overseas.

The Pleasure Gardens of Marylebone & Vauxhall, London, England, were among England's first sites of light musical

Halifax's Capitol Theatre with its striking medieval castle theme

entertainment and were popular places on summer evenings. The gardens had the same escapist feeling for the patrons. The leading exponent of the atmospheric theatre in England was Theodore Komisarjevsky. Originally a stage designer, Komisarjevsky later branched out into designing theatre auditoriums. He sensed that theatre patrons desired a certain romance that the atmospheric theatre would provide. His most interesting theatres were the Granadas at Woolwich and Tooting and the Astorias of Finsbury Park and Streatham.

The Capitol was built on the site where Lord Cornwallis founded Halifax in 1749.

The Granada Theatre in Tooting (a suburb of London, England) is an unusual atmospheric built in a combination of art moderne and high Gothic style, the British version of "The Cathedral of the Motion Picture."

The ultimate atmospheric, however, was to be found not in North America or in England, but in the tropics. In Half-Way-Tree, a suburb of Kingston, Jamaica, the lovely Odeon-Half-Way-Tree stood open with two enormous palm trees, one on each side of the stage, piercing the real tropical night sky. If it rained the audience had to crowd in underneath the balcony, but it almost never rains at night in Half-Way-Tree! The stage was equipped with house and travelling curtains. The side walls were beautifully designed and the screen was large, but many could not resist lifting their eyes from the screen to the magnificent stars, directly overhead.

Vaudeville was wounded by the introduction of movies that people actually wanted to see, and it was further doomed by elaborate shows in elaborate theatres. In addition to stage shows, talking movies were the final blow. The eight-act vaudeville show was outdated and eclipsed, and so was the theatre it played in. Larger movie palaces, "cathedrals of the motion picture," were waiting in the wings.

The lovely little Port Hope (Ontario) Capitol, now the Port Hope Festival Theatre, was, and remains, a gem of its type, where patrons are transported back to a medieval town. One of two atmospheric theatres still operating in Canada, its marquee proudly proclaims that it is Canada's most beautiful theatre.

The Montreal Capitol was truly a cathedral of the motion picture. It had one of the most elaborate coffered ceilings of any theatre in North America. Giant Corinthian columns lining the walls and organ pipes rising out of the box seats were among its most attractive decorative features.

3 THE CATHEDRAL OF THE MOTION PICTURE

Everything about the movie palace was extravagant and overpowering. While the atmospheric movie palace has a discernible tradition within theatre design, the hard-top movie palace is something unique. It is a perfect reflection of its times—the daring, wild, imaginative decade of the twenties. There could never be too much gilt, lacquer, paint, cut glass, mirrors, chandeliers, carvings or velvet. No show could be too elaborate or use too many stage effects.

Hollywood was on every main street in North America thanks to American movie producers and American movie theatre architects, but the movie palace was found only in the larger centres. It was very special and carried a higher price of admission. Absolutely everything was done on a grand scale in the movie palace. It was for the movie palaces that the "presentation policy" was established. This meant that the stage show was created to complement the movie, and original music was composed to add to the overall theme. These special unit stage shows were then sent around the circuits to coincide with particular movies.

There is no dictionary definition for a movie palace. Many great theatres which showed both movies and live shows together were not movie palaces. It comes down to size. The real movie palace had over 3,000 seats, an elevator for the

Loew's Theatre in Montreal had a magnificent proscenium arch over which horses seemed to be racing the sunrise.

orchestra and revolving, elevator-equipped stages. Using this definition, Canada did not have a single movie palace—nor for that matter did Britain, Australia or Europe. The movie palace was an American phenomenon, copied in other countries on a smaller scale.

It is rather odd that the world famous Grauman's Chinese Theatre in Hollywood (now Mann's Chinese Theatre) probably the best-known movie theatre in the world, is too small at 2,300 seats to be classed as a true American movie palace. But there is no doubt that what went on at Grauman's made it every inch a movie palace. According to California theatre historian Terry Helgessen, the stage was 165 feet wide and 48 feet deep. In one show finale, 75 girls in Louis XVI costumes and wigs walked down several staircases into a reflecting pool and disappeared! Seemingly underwater, they changed costumes only to reappear wearing pearl-studded leotards and elaborate headresses. The girls then climbed the staircases highlighted by 21 fountains, all spraying water at

Grauman's Chinese Theatre is arguably the most famous movie theatre in the world. Its forecourt, where celebrities place their hand prints in wet cement, was Syd Grauman's most successful publicity gimmick. The idea came from Mary Pickford, one of the partners who financed its construction.

different levels. Bright-coloured spots cross-lit the water giving the effect of a million, coloured jewels being sprayed over the stage. But it was the forecourt of Grauman's theatre that made it and Grauman famous. It was here that the stars placed their hands and feet in a slab of wet cement.

The American movie palaces were built mainly between the years 1919 and 1929, before the Depression and before sound came to the movies. Although Canadian theatres never seemed to be as big or as fantastically decorated as the American movie palaces, they were nonetheless quite large and beautiful. They were also, for the most part, built before the American theatres. Shea's Hippodrome in Toronto (about 3,000 seats) was built in

Shea's Hippodrome Theatre, Toronto, was one of the largest vaudeville theatres in the world when it opened in 1914—just about as large as theatres could be in the days before microphones.

1914. A first-class vaudeville theatre, it offered "Keith and Albee Big-Time Vaudeville" and operated successfully for many years. As the public's taste in entertainment changed, the theatre's management altered its show policy.

Izz Gang describes a night in 1925 at the height of the popularity of the presentation policy: "In the mid-twenties, that Golden Age of the silent movie, Shea's Hippodrome might have a bill like this: Overture–Selections from Faust–News of the Week –Comedy–Charlie Chaplin in The Cure–Novelette –the Mighty Wurlitzer. Then the Prologue before the Feature Presentation, "Lon Chaney" in *The Phantom of the Opera*." (Shea's Buffalo and dozens of big theatres all over the world might have had the same programme.)

As crowds rushed through the door, their tickets were taken by Teddy Gee, resplendent in a colourful but dignified uniform. Izz Gang recalls what it was like to enter the Hippodrome in the twenties,

> *The feature film is nearing its end so there is time to look up at the impressive curved sweep of the balcony front. We enjoyed the pulsating lights behind the semi-circular grills fronting the organ chambers above the box seats, as one after another the vertical shutters opened to allow more sound to pour from the chambers as well as more light.*

Advertisement for the big-time vaudeville show at Shea's Hippodrome

The 12 opera boxes in Shea's Hippodrome offered a wonderfully intimate view of the big stage.

Musicians are filing into the orchestra pit from doors under the stage; music stand lights wink on, one by one, and the conductor comes to stand in the centre as "The End" first flashes onto the screen, then onto the curtains converging grandly from left to right. Instruments zero in to synchronize with the pitch of the English horn and the evening's performance is about to begin. [That 24-piece symphony orchestra and the overture must have thrilled the audience almost as much as the film.]

Imagine then a medley of Spanish melodies when Valentino's Blood and Sand was featured, or Ketelby's music, "In a Persian Market," was heard to anticipate Douglas Fairbank's Thief of Bagdad. With the applause following the overture, the newsreel would flash onto the curtain as it was being parted and the orchestra would settle in to provide incidental music for the half dozen or so items portraying newsworthy events around the world. Appropriate music was remarkably timed to accent each event. For example, funeral accompaniment ended with the completion of a news item relating to some VIP's funeral, and if the next title announced a *recent marine disaster, the orchestra immediately began to imitate a howling storm at sea.*

After the last newsreel item, the comedy title brought a musical change. Musicians' lights blinked off as they vanished under the stage and the organ console platform rose to provide the bold and blazing sounds flooding out of the organ chambers.

To fill out the programme, a novelty was often inserted between comedy and prologue. This might be anything from a sing-along or cartoon, to an organ interlude. One outstanding novelty was the three-dimensional experience where the projection machine threw separate red and green images onto the screen, slightly displaced. By viewing the screen through red and green transparencies, one had a stereoscopic thrill watching the dizzying pace of a roller coaster.

Izz Gang recalled one memorable November evening in 1925 when Shea's showed *The Phantom of the Opera*. It opened with a marvellous scene of some great views of the audience in the Paris Opera House. (These colourful scenes were filmed in the days when each of the 35 millimetre frames was laboriously tinted by hand, the Technicolour of the time.)

It didn't take much imagination to substitute The Hippodrome for the Paris Opera House except for one missing object—the ill-fated chandelier! Yet, with some imagination, you could transform the coffered circle glowing, halo-like into that pendant chandelier!

More memorable was the unmasking scene when, after a tortured night of disturbing dreams and ominous forebodings, Christine entered the Phantom's living room. Then, on the silent screen, Lon Chaney seated himself at the organ console. At this time the sound of the theatre orchestra faded and the mighty theatre organ took over playing the haunting bars of "Don Juan Triumphant" while the orchestra had a few seconds of rest. Just before the Phantom's mask was dropped the music of both the orchestra and the organ grew louder and then the great organ was played with all the stops out at full volume at the moment when Chaney's hideously disfigured face dominated the screen. The effect was so overwheming that the audience's gasp of horror was completely drowned out!

The "Hipp" was one of the largest vaudeville theatres in the world and was one of the Big Four, in terms of size and quality of shows. (The Hipp presented live shows even as late as the 1940s.) The other members of the Big Four were The Orpheum in L.A., Loew's State and the Palace in New York City.

Izz Gang tells of special atmospheric projectors being used on a cyclorama at Shea's Theatre (usually, cycloramas were used for sky effects on stage). It seemed amazing to him, considering that the projection equipment was in the wings, that the projected clouds, which drifted all the way across the entire space, never went out of focus. Apparently the company that serviced the equipment was under such an exclusive contract that nobody was allowed to see inside one of these machines to see how it worked.

Shea's Hippodrome Theatre, even in the days before air conditioning, never seemed to get too hot even on the warmest days. Perhaps the building's great height and size helped, as hot

Shea's Hippodrome made use of hundreds of decorative lights placed in elaborate plaster mouldings. This was quite unusual in a theatre built before 1915.

air was exhausted through the roof. In addition, perfume was sprayed in front of the fans to make the theatre seem more elegant. Al Lowery of Orillia, Ontario does not remember the Shea's as being all that cool. One day that will remain forever in his memory, was a hot one for him. He was servicing the console on the Wurlitzer organ during a sound movie. The organ was hidden in a little space in the lowest part of the orchestra pit where there was very little air. He stripped down to his underwear to keep from expiring altogether, and was more or less draped over the keyboard when he suddenly noticed it was not so dark down there anymore. Unknowingly, he had accidentally pushed the button that started the elevator to take the organ to its highest position. There he was, exposed to a stunned audience! He could not press the descend button fast enough. The "damn thing seemed to take forever," he recalled.

The Hippodrome's large stage featured the greatest stars and biggest shows Toronto had ever seen. Its show policy attracted the greatest acts in the business, making "The Hipp" one of North America's "Big Four" vaudeville theatres.

Marion Hanna, who was an usherette at three of Toronto's theatres, remembers Shea's with particular fondness. She recalls that it had eight of the best vaudeville acts in Toronto— the biggest shows with the best stars staged in the most elaborate ways.

> *It was the most professional of all the theatres to work for because the people who put on the shows were so dedicated and demanding. Jack Arthur was the orchestra leader. He was very particular about all the arrangements, not just musically but on stage as well. Midge, his wife, was also a very professional person. Some of the actors could be quite difficult to work with, temperamental and dictatorial. Harry Lauder, was one of the more difficult ones to appear at Shea's, while Carmen Miranda, who was a big hit, was not at all difficult.*

The most spectacular show Marion saw was the stage and screen production of *The Ten Commandments* (the silent version). "There seemed to be hundreds of people on the stage and lots of spectacle with lightning, thunder and wind. Despite all of this nothing ever seemed to go wrong, all the special effects always seemed to work perfectly." Marion recalls one of the particularly beautiful girls at Shea's, Dorothy Flood, who used to dress in a lively Japanese costume and serve tea in the afternoons in the theatre's mezzanine lobby. As patrons came up the stairs she would graciously invite them to have tea and biscuits in the stuffed wicker chairs. The Shea's Hippodrome did have style.

The Hippodrome featured both the stage &
screen versions of The Ten Commandments.

The name "hippodrome" was probably taken from the famous New York Hippodrome of 1905. This theatre was the largest in the world at the time and certainly had the most spectacular shows in America, such as elaborately staged circus acts with elephants and horses. There was even a small lake in front of the stage into which real horses plunged, only to swim away under the stage. This spine-tingling sight thrilled everybody so much that each time it happened the audience of 5,000 rose to their feet.

Box seats at Shea's Hippodrome.

Another Hippodrome built in Paris, in 1910, was also known for staging spectacles. It later converted to movies and has the reputation of being the world's first palatial movie theatre. It had rear projection to thrill its audience of 5,000. When the name Hippodrome became dated, it was changed to the Paris Gaumont. Similarly, in Toronto, Shea's Hippodrome, affectionately known as the "Hipp," later became known as the Shea's.

In 1919, Thomas Lamb built the world's largest theatre and ultimate movie palace, the 5,300 seat Capitol in New York. The auditorium of the Capitol was magnificent. The style was Robert Adam and Empire complete with damask hangings, bas relief carvings, silver leaf and classical columns. The lobby had a white marble staircase, rock crystal chandeliers and mahogany panelling.

One of the more unusual stars to appear on the Capitol's stage was Sister Aimee Semple McPherson from Ingersoll, Ontario, later of Hollywood's Gospel Circuit. Her appearance at the Capitol came right after her scandalous divorce and the sensational trial over her "kidnapping." At one time, there were hundreds of gospel temples in her "circuit." (Actress Faye Dunaway portrayed her in one of the Hollywood movies that

The New York Capitol was the world's largest when it opened. It was designed by Thomas Lamb, the same architect who designed the Toronto Pantages which opened less than a year later.

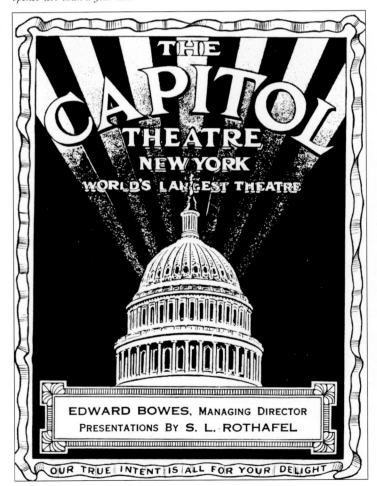

THE CAPITOL THEATRE NEW YORK
WORLD'S LARGEST THEATRE

EDWARD BOWES, MANAGING DIRECTOR
PRESENTATIONS BY S. L. ROTHAFEL

OUR TRUE INTENT IS ALL FOR YOUR DELIGHT

depicted Sister Aimee's life.) Aimee was very familiar with what worked as theatre and what did not. She dressed heself in a sheer white satin gown with full-length sleeves for her appearance at the Capitol. She alone occupied the great stage while a single soft spotlight shone down on her. When she raised her arms so that they were parallel to the floor, she looked like a living cross. But the New York sinners stayed away in droves, their chance at redemption gone.

Thomas Lamb is the best-known architect of the hard-top movie palace. Born in Scotland, he emigrated first to Canada and then to the United States. Most of his early buildings were designed in the northeast for the Loew's vaudeville circuit. The Loew's Winter Garden in Toronto was one of his earliest. He also did some work for the Poli circuit before it was taken over by Loew's, and he designed the lovely Capitol in Brantford, Ontario, his only theatre that was not, at least before 1920, part of a huge circuit.

Lamb produced many of America's great movie palaces including the Capitol and the Strand in New York, the Fox in San Francisco (considered to be his masterpiece), the Ohio in Columbus and others in the United States, Canada, England, Australia, India, Egypt and Africa. His early neoclassical designs were inspired by Robert Adam and featured columns and domes. They soon gave way to just about every style imaginable, including the atmospheric. He blended many styles into what always became a building of elegance and style. From the baroque and rococo through to Art Deco and Art Moderne, he was respected for his treatment of them all. Thomas Lamb died

Evangelist Aimee Semple McPherson from Ingersoll, Ontario, later of Hollywood's Gospel Circuit, made an appearance at the New York Capitol, but sinners stayed away in droves.

Thomas Lamb was perhaps the world's best-known movie palace architect, and one of the most prolific.

in 1942. It is doubtful if any other architect has thrilled as many people with his buildings, and sad that so few of the millions of viewers who sat enthralled in his theatres ever knew his name.

Lamb built many beautiful theatres in Canada, opening three of them—Canada's largest and finest showplaces—in 1920: the Pantages in Toronto (3,626 seats); Loew's Uptown in Toronto (3,000 seats); and Loew's Capitol in Ottawa (2,580 seats). Many feel that the smallest of the three was the most beautiful and that it had the grandest split staircase and lobby anywhere.

Ottawa's Capitol saw as many stars and as many shows as any movie theatre anywhere in the world. Since Ottawa had no "National Theatre," the Capitol offered a great variety of stage and screen performances every year until it was torn down in 1970. In 1935, the National Symphony Orchestra of Washington appeared at the Capitol, in 1936 the Toronto symphony Orchestra and in 1937 the big band sound was featured in a "Swing Night." Nelson Eddy appeared on stage in 1938 and in 1939, Ethel Barrymore starred in *Whiteoaks*, a great Canadian play. John Gielgud appeared in *Love is Love* and Michael Redgrave thrilled audiences in *Macbeth*. The Metropolitan Opera Company of New York performed there, as did the Sadlers Wells, Marion Anderson, William Warfield, Victor Borge, the Peking Opera Company, Pearl Bailey, Nat King Cole, Gracie Fields, Jose Greco, and a host of others.

Like all theatres, the Capitol faced a dilemma with the introduction of sound movies. In 1928, the Capitol announced that the theatre would be wired for sound. The statement was

The wonderful Majestic Theatre of San Antonio Texas was the epitome of the atmospheric movie theatre. It transported the audience to an exotic Spanish garden beneath a star-filled sky. It was built in 1929 by John Eberson, the king of atmospheric architects.

The lovely Capitol in Port Hope, Ontario was nowhere near the size of the San Antonio Majestic but it is a gem of its type. Here patrons are taken to a medieval town in Europe. It is one of only two atmospheric theatres still operating in Canada.

Classic marbleized columns adorned with cameo-shaped ornaments and fanciful capitals graced the Montreal Granada.
The lovely, curved balustrade over the columns also shows a wonderful attention to detail.

Meticulous detail was rendered in many
parts of Toronto's Runnymede Theatre. (Top
left) complicated plaster lattice-work which
allowed the sound from the organ pipes to
enter the auditorium;
Top right) flower designs over the tops of
false pillars
Centre) angels, birds and shell designs
found under the atmospheric ceiling.

Below left) The Capitol, Cornwall, Ont.
Below right) The moon, clouds and stars
drifted by on the ceiling of the Capitol, just
as they did in the Runnymede, its near-t...

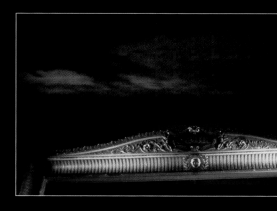

Toronto's famed Winter Garden was a precursor to the atmospheric theatre. It was designed to resemble a roof-top garden and was inspired by the "pleasure gardens" and winter gardens of the British legitimate theatre.

The Winter Garden moon peeks through tree branches which frame the stage and reach up into the plaster sky of the sounding board.

Elgin Theatre, Toronto

The Ottawa Capitol likely had the most magnificent staircase of any theatre in Canada. This theatre was considered by some to be the finest of Thomas Lamb's Canadian designs. The auditorium closely resembled the Toronto Pantages which also opened in 1920.

The Imperial Theatre, Saint John N.B. which opened in 1913, has been saved from the wrecking ball. It has been beautifully restored and over the years has attracted some big names including Sir Harry Lauder, Ethel Barrymore, Sir John Martin Harvey, Burns and Allen and Gracie Fields.

The Capitol in Moncton, N.B. has one of the most attractive stages and house curtains of any theatre in Canada. David Hannivan of Hannivan and Co., restoration experts, claims the painted stencil work is as beautiful as can be found anywhere.

The Quebec Capitole also has a charming small hotel with about forty rooms located over the grand lobby. This theatre with its unusual curved façade and French baroque roof is one-of-a-kind in Canada.

The Capitole in Quebec City was not only saved but has also been restored and transformed so that it is actually far more attractive than it was before. The building also houses a restaurant off the main lobby with a lovely sidewalk cafe.

The Haskell Opera House sits astride the border of two countries! This unusual situation has led to endless complications over the years with customs officials. When this beautiful theatre was being restored, permits and regulations had to satisfy both countries. Some of the supplies had to be flown in and dropped into the theatre by helicopter to simplify things. "Hassles at the Haskell" is a light-hearted show that never ends. The wonderful Venetian scene painted on the asbestos curtain was typical of those found in town halls and opera houses across North America.

The detailed paint over the proscenium arch were as grand any found in much larger theatres.

Vaulted ceiling, the Pantages, Toronto

Capitol Theatre, Moncton

The Winter Garden, Toronto

Plaster detail, the Elgin, Toronto

The great crystal chandelier adorning the centre of the dome in the Ottawa Capitol was one of Thomas Lamb's trademarks.

Mural of dancing nymphs on the sounding board of the Sanderson Centre, Brantford, Ontario

The magnificent house curtain in the Loew's Theatre (Elgin) Toronto was hand crafted by the scenic artist, A. Howard.

The rotunda of the Allen Theatre, Cleveland Ohio, is one of the most elegant to be found in North America. This theatre was one of the finest ever built by the Allen Theatre Circuit of Canada. The circuit was squeezed out of the U.S. market and its nearly fifty Canadian theatres were taken over by Famous Players. The recently restored Allen is now the proud centrepiece of the renowned Cleveland Playhouse Square, one of the largest

The Orpheum in Vancouver is one of the bright spots in the history of Canada's theatres. Built in 1927, the magnificent 2,788-seat theatre was rescued by the people of Vancouver in 1975. It was one of the first major theatres to be saved in Canada and is now the home of the Vancouver Symphony Orchestra.

The Imperial Theatre in Montreal is the only large metropolitan theatre preserved by Famous Players of Canada. For years it was the home of blockbuster movies, but it has since closed. This grand old theatre is waiting to spring to life once again.

The Colossus, Toronto, is Famous Players' version of a movie palace for the year 2000. On a site near two super highways, this megaplex theatre resembles a giant spacecraft and appeals to a young audience.

Victoria's Royal Theatre is a jewel. It hosts the Victoria Symphony Orchestra, the Pacific Opera Victoria in addition to a diverse selection of cultural fare.

The Capitol Theatre, Brantford, Ontario, first
called the Temple and now The Sanderson Centre
for the Performing Arts, was one of the earliest large
theatres built for the Allen Circuit. This beautifully
restored theatre was built in 1919 by world famous
movie palace architect, Thomas Lamb and was one
of his earliest Canadian creations.

The unusual proscenium arch at the
Imperial in Saint John, N.B. appeared as
if it was a giant emerald and gold necklace.

Many feel the Ottawa Capitol was the most attractive of all of Lamb's theatres.

The magnificent split staircase in the Ottawa Capitol was built in the grand movie palace tradition.

retracted under pressure from the Musicians' Union but that only slowed the process down. The last regularly scheduled silent movie was *Marquee Preferred* (1929) starring Adolphe Menjou, while the first sound movie was *Syncopation* with Fred Waring's Pennsylvanians. There were also five acts of vaudeville and the orchestra played at all three shows.

Change was inevitable. In the fall of 1930, the orchestra sat silently in the orchestra pit during the movies. They sat there for six weeks without playing a note. In 1931, the theatre was renovated and re-opened as the RKO Capitol under the joint ownership of RKO and Famous Players Canadian Corporation. The Capitol continued its lavish and varied programmes after it was renovated.

Sadly the theatre closed in 1970. The last show was a special screening of Mary Pickford's *Pollyanna* and a benefit stage show

The Pantages' enormous 3,626-seat auditorium.

which played to a packed house. It seems a shame that the theatre was destroyed to make room for an office building and two or three ugly little cinemas.

It is odd that Toronto's Pantages Theatre, which was built in the same year as the Ottawa Capitol and was the largest Pantages theatre anywhere, had a stage reputation which paled in comparison to the Ottawa Capitol. An advertisement in the *Toronto Star* of August 28, 1920, heralded Canada's largest new showplace:

TO-NIGHT AT THE PANTAGES THEATRE

A new page will be written in Toronto's theatrical history, and for a long time to come, thousands upon thousands will comment upon the wondrous beauty of this exquisite palace of amusement.

To help in to-night's dedication exercise Montagu Love and Mildred Harris Chaplin have journeyed to Toronto to lend their services on this occasion.

To-night at 6:30 about 600 seats will be placed on sale for those who cannot gain admission. 25¢ before 5:00, 45¢ after 5:00.

The Pantages' grand house curtain was said to be designed by a Russian artist who was inspired by Maeterlinck's "The Bluebird."

Even on the Pantages' opening night, its bill paled. At a competing theatre across town, direct from the Century Theatre in New York and from His Majesty's Theatre in London, Chu Chin Chow was packing them in with a cast of 300 people.

Although the opening show for the Pantages was perhaps not the most spectacular Toronto had ever seen, people were impressed with the theatre and its 22,500 square feet. The huge house curtain with its big pelmet (swag drapes under the arch) was supposedly a replica of the newly-opened Capitol in New York City and was designed by a young Russian artist, so it was said, inspired by Maeterlinck's "The Bluebird." The entire theatre was done in tones of blue and gold. Pantages was advertised as "one of North America's most beautiful theatres, done in an Adam's style with Georgian architecture and lots of real antiques." Its long lobby and entranceway actually led to the street behind the one on which the theatre front was located, so that the bulk of the building sat on cheaper land. The Uptown in Toronto also used this technique as did several others in Canada.

Chu Chin Chow boasted 14 scenes and a company of 300 people. The show drew large crowds across town.

Canada's largest theatre, the Pantages in Toronto was the largest in the Pantages circuit, including the famous Hollywood Pantages.

The auditoriums of all three theatres—the Toronto Pantages, the Uptown and the Ottawa Capitol—were very similar. If they were not all decorated in different colours, one might easily have become confused as to which was which. They were all built in the grand opera house style with domes, box seats and chandeliers. Lamb also used many of the typical Adam style motifs. Arabesque panels, urns, swags, cameos, medallions, bell flowers, various plaster friezes showing nymphs and dancing figures, cherubs, putti and several kinds of bas relief sculpture, especially the lyre and other musical instruments, were just some of the elaborate designs found in Lamb's theatres.

The Pantages was Canada's first movie theatre to be equipped with a cinemascope screen and its regular gigantic screen saw many a movie premiere.

The grand lobby entrance of the Pantages Theatre, Toronto. This long lobby stretches nearly half a block and leads up and over an alley separating the theatre's entrance on Yonge Street from the cheaper land on Victoria Street on which the main theatre was actually built.

Ceiling detail

Orchestra level at the Pantages

Even the wash-room vestibules were elegant at the Pantages.

This view of the Hamilton Pantages shows some of the thousands of seats awaiting patrons.

Kathleen Stokes, Canada's most famous female theatre organist, was much sought after, but was most often heard at Toronto's Loew's theatres and The Imperial (formerly the Pantages).

The theatre was packing them in for *The Godfather* when it was torn apart to become the Imperial Six. The Pantages was born again after an infusion of $18 million by Cineplex Odeon Corporation and opened with a spectacular production of *The Phantom Of The Opera*. This production was so successful that it ran for more than ten years and repaid the cost of renovating the theatre many times over. The Pantages was the largest private restoration in North America.

Toronto Loew's Uptown Theatre, which was quite similar to the Montreal Loew's, had an auditorium 120 feet by 145 feet with a beautiful Japanese setting on its stage. Canada's famous theatre organist Kathleen Stokes loved the Loew's and Loew's Uptown theatres even though, on one memorable occasion, things did not go well. It was the night of her debut. Mice had munched on parts of the organ wiring and entered the organ console. While she was playing they scampered across the keyboard causing some frantic fingering by the diminutive organist, and certainly not augmenting the music. Then, at the finale, she pulled out all the stops and as the organ reached a great crescendo, many of the footlights shattered with a great crash sending flying glass all over the stage (courtesy of a short-circuit caused by the hungry mice.)

Marion Hanna, who was an avid showgoer as well as an usherette, remembers seeing Mary Pickford at the Pantages (then called the Imperial): "What struck me was how tiny her figure appeared to be on that big stage! Seeing her in closeups on the high and wide screen first made her seem all the smaller. It sure made the title of 'Little Mary' all the more meaningful."

Toronto Loew's Uptown, another Thomas Lamb movie palace, was the second largest of the five large Lamb theatres built in Canada. With 3,000 seats it was still smaller than the 3,626-seat Pantages.

Hanna recalls that there was a great camaraderie among theatre personnel: "We never had to pay to get into a show. Jack Arthur and his choreographer Leon Leonidoff, who had earlier worked at the Shea's and the Tivoli, were now performing at the Loew's Uptown, so we often went to see them there. Their staging was as good as ever, but the stars of the shows and the part of the show that came from New York just seemed to be inferior to what was done at Shea's."

Leon Leonidoff, the dance choreographer at the Uptown, pioneered some wonderful dance ideas and went on to become famous. He, along with Jack Arthur, developed the idea of a chorus line composed of girls all the same height doing a precision dance number with the kick-line as the finish. About 1930, Leonidoff and Arthur were both invited to try out at the world's largest theatre, the famous Roxy of New York. The Roxy had

The spacious auditorium at Loew's London Theatre. Many of its design features were similar to those of the Pantages and other larger theatres built throughout the world.

The long entrance at Loew's, highlighted with a row of crystal chandeliers and mirrors, led Londoners to an elegant auditorium built on the street behind.

6,200 seats and a fantastic stage. Leonidoff went, Jack Arthur didn't. While there, Leonidoff formed the Roxyettes and later, along with Russell Markert, he went over to the new Radio City Music Hall (also billed as the world's largest theatre with 6,200 seats) and formed the famous Rockettes.

Until sound was added to movies, the movie theatre stage was an exciting place. The 1920s in Canada saw all kinds of variety, but the production of stage shows ended after 1928. The great Radio City Music Hall in New York continued with its stage show policy, the rare exception to what was happening elsewhere in the world.

The New York Roxy was the world's largest and most expensive movie palace when it opened in 1927. Samuel Roxy (born Samuel Rothefel) became a household word all over the United States, Canada, England, Europe, and even Australia. The theatre was designed by Walter W. Ahschlager of Chicago in conjunction with professional theatre decorator, Harold W. Rambusch. It had a rotunda the size of a railroad station.

The Roxy Theatre was advertised as "the cathedral of the motion picture" and it is possible that this title upset a lot of people. There were some cultural wags who described this cathedral as a cathedral of sin built by the devil himself. They thought that sinful bishops might appear at any moment from green-coloured niches in the walls or from behind amber and green-coloured lights which played beyond the organ grills, as the devil himself played some abomination on the so-called cathedral organ. But this was not the effect that the Roxy had on the public. It was designed for the great masses of the city of New York and they reacted exactly the way the architects had hoped.

The enormous Roxy theatre stage was set low so that no matter where one sat in the auditorium, one looked down on the stage, never up. It was divided into four sections, two of

The 6,000-seat New York Roxy was advertised as the world's largest theatre.

which were on elevators. Complete sets were designed and built so that they could be changed in 20 seconds. At the rear of the stage was an enormous cyclorama designed to diffuse sound, and when properly lit, to give the effect of a sky. It weighed over ten tons but could be lifted with the ease of a sheet of paper. The stage also had a system of traps which made it possible to change parts of scenery with machine-gun rapidity. The great house curtain was designed to give various tableau effects, and it could be gathered, parted or lifted in sections to give many varied maskings of the stage. There were four conductors for the Roxy musicians and a music library of 10,000 numbers and 50,000 orchestrations. Three immense organ consoles were designed to be played simultaneously by three organists!

Roxy, the man, went on to even greater things than the Roxy Theatre. An advertisement in the New York papers in 1932 states "To the hands of Roxy, master showman, RKO entrusts the two Radio City theatres, Radio City Music Hall and the new RKO Roxy!" Radio City Music Hall was originally to be called the International Music Hall but the name was changed before it opened in deference to NBC. The RKO Roxy (later the Center Theatre) was a considerably smaller theatre but very beautiful. With its elegant wood in the auditorium, many felt it was far more attractive than Radio City Music Hall.

Radio City Music Hall uses plaster, rather than wood, for dramatic effect. The Art Deco walls of the theatre can be lit in different colours to match the musical moods coming from the stage. A typical stage show requires about 180 performers and backstage people. The theatre has four backstage elevators, three elevated stages and the largest Wurlitzer theatre organ in the world. A band car on an enormous electric lift enables

Marquee at Radio City Music Hall.

the symphony orchestra to rise and descend dramatically from above, below and to the rear of the main stage. Perhaps the most noticeable feature of the auditorium is its enormous two-ton contoured curtain which, like the Roxy's, can be sculpted in different ways to frame the stage opening.

Since its opening on December 27, 1932, well over 230 million people have visited Radio City Music Hall. The last scheduled show in the Spring of 1979 was an emotional and memorable event. During the final standing ovation, the ushers could not get to the Rockettes to give them each a

Radio City Music Hall boasted three elevated stages and an enormous turntable on stage. A $70 million restoration project in 1999 returned the Manhattan landmark to its 1930s art deco splendour.

Buddy Rogers at Loew's Theatre, Toronto.

bouquet of roses so they threw them, one after the other. It became a rain of roses and for once, that slick line of girls broke ranks! It was a thrilling and poignant moment, because nobody knew then that the "greatest theatre in the world" was soon to be saved. Although it no longer shows movies on a regular basis, its magnificent stage is used for lavish shows.

The concept of the presentation house and the movie palace worked well when movies were silent and all the music came live from the theatre. When sound movies came in, it no longer worked. Even the tiniest theatre could have a "presentation" on the screen—"all singing, all dancing." With the exception of Radio City Music Hall, the American movie palaces only lasted from about 1920 to 1928. Then they were no longer built. The stage and screen shows of the big band era were their last hurrah.

The big band era lasted about ten years and was ideal for great movie palaces like the New York Paramount. The Casa Loma Orchestra (of Toronto's Casa Loma fame) played there to great success. Audiences loved the music of the big bands as much as they did the movies. Buddy Rogers, star of *Wings* and many other films, broke the house record at the Paramount, with his own orchestra. Buddy has mentioned that playing the New York Paramount was one of the most exhausting dates he has ever played. Seven one-hour shows a day would surely tax anyone! Buddy Rogers was as famous as any of the band leaders featured in the big band era. (Buddy was married to Mary Pickford for many years. On May 16, 1983, he unveiled a statue of Mary at the site of her birthplace in Toronto.)

The Ottawa Capitol, Vancouver Capitol, Pantages, Loew's Uptown and Loew's Montreal may not have had revolving and elevated stages, nor could they pack 30,000 people into a single theatre in a single day (seven shows a day), but they did hold about 20,000 people in a day and produced some terrific shows, and some wonderful memories. This was the moneymaking idea behind the concept of the movie palace. Fill the place. Entertain the masses.

Casa Loma, Canada's most famous "castle," gave its name to the famed "Casa Loma Orchestra." At the height of the big-band era the Orchestra packed the great New York Paramount several times a day.

Trois Rivière's Capitol. Its large auditorium has many of the decorative elements of much larger Montreal theatres —the decorator, Emmanuel Briffa, worked on most of Quebec's grand theatres and many in the rest of Canada as well as some in the United States. When the theatre was slated to be twinned, the people of Trois Rivières swung into action and the city acquired it. The lovely auditorium has been completely restored.

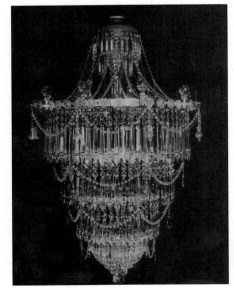

This magnificent chandelier is still a feature at the Capitol.

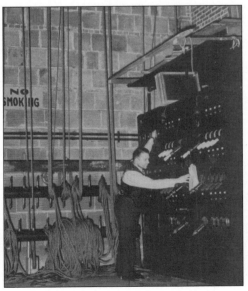

This rare backstage shot shows a typical 1930s lighting panel. Note: the hemp rope and pin rail system used to fly the scenery.

Built in 1927-28 by Jean Baptiste Robert, the Capitol remained in the Robert family until it was purchased by the United Amusement Company in 1966. In the 1960s, the United Amusement Company controlled almost every important movie theatre in Quebec. (It was an arm of Famous Players.)

The original box office of the Capitol illustrates the attention given to detail found throughout the theatre.

Sincerely Yours
Kathleen Stokes
Imperial Theatre

4 THE MIGHTY WURLITZER

In those wonderful days of silent pictures, the mighty Wurlitzer made all the difference as to whether an audience liked a movie or not. The Wurlitzer organ that appeared mysteriously from the walls on Radio City Music Hall's opening night in 1932 was the ultimate theatre organ. This incredible instrument sported two consoles played simultaneously by two different organists. Its 58 sets of pipes have never been out-ranked by any theatre organ installation. The organ has a sound equal in value to pipes 64 feet long. There are 455 sets of pipes.

Whether in the Fox Theatre in Detroit, the Orpheum in Vancouver, the Odeon Marble Arch in London or the State in Melbourne, the sound of thousands of theatre organ pipes had the same effect. Movie palace audiences loved it. Today, there are associations all over the world with hundreds of members devoted to saving and reconditioning theatre organs.

The console of a great theatre organ looks almost as complicated as the cockpit of a modern jet. Played well, a good theatre organ made all the difference to a silent film. A theatre organist could actually make or break a picture.

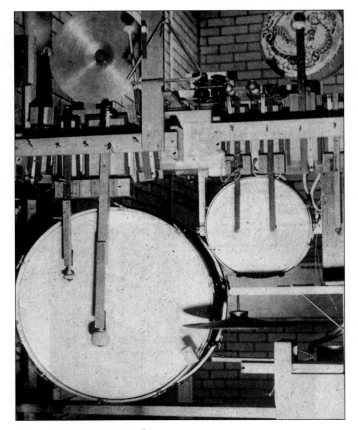

Percussion instruments inside an organ. The organ not only presented music, but also produced all the important sound effects.

Crowds still line up to hear the Vancouver Orpheum's Wurlitzer on the rare occasions when it is played.

The great theatre organ was not just a musical instrument. Capable of sounding like thunder or imitating a violin, it was an entire sound effects department! There were stops to imitate the sound of waves lapping on the seashore (made by the organ's sandblocks); there were fire sirens, car horns, steamship whistles, imitations of rain on the roof, galloping horses and just about everything else one could imagine. Barbara Woffindin, now 103 years old, vividly remembers going to her first moving picture in Brantford. It was a short newsreel of Queen Victoria's funeral, and the mournful clop of the horses' hooves on the cobblestones made a very strong impression.

The Wurlitzer could even produce a slap in the face and the sound of smashing crockery. (The latter was done with bits of metal plates strung on wires so they could be made to drop onto a sounding plate when the organist touched the appropriate button.) One stop, called a diaphone, was so loud that it could be heard for miles and was actually purchased by the Canadian Government and used as a foghorn. The very latest digital sound systems in today's stadium-type megaplexes cannot duplicate the tremendous sound and vibration made by the diaphone. This was one organ stop that could make your bones vibrate!

When a silent movie was flickering on the screen and everybody was overacting, the Wurlitzer organ, the Moller organ, the Kimble organ, or whichever organ was being played, helped to make the movie a success. A good organist could make or break a silent film. Theatre organs were nearly always called Wurlitzers whether they were or not. Canada's largest theatre, the Imperial, had a Warren. All theatre organs had snare drums, bass drums, glockenspiels, marimbas, xylophones and even phantom grand pianos. A real grand piano usually sat by itself on stage, its keyboard activated by the organist's console.

Most of the theatre organ effects were developed by a man named Hope Jones. He was an eccentric genius who designed the "unit orchestra" organ. The unit orchestra was a system of pipe unification. Hope Jones developed an "organ manual" (keyboards) which could play several ranks of pipes at the same time and made it possible for each rank of pipes to be played from each keyboard at different octave pitches. This allowed a small six-rank organ, that is, an organ with six sets of pipes, to outshine or outplay a church organ requiring thirty ranks. And so it was not just the sound effects of the unit organ, it was also the volume and quantity of sound that distinguished it from a church organ.

Hope Jones, inventor

Rudolph Wurlitzer

The biggest theatre organ is not even in a theatre. It is the Barton organ in Chicago Stadium. This monster has only six keyboards but its enormous wind pressure makes the 5,000 pipes sound like an army of musicians. The world's biggest straight (non-unified) concert organ is the incredible Midler-Loche organ in Atlantic City Auditorium. Its 33,112 pipes cost $3.5 million dollars to construct back in 1928 and require a crew of 2 or 3 technicians just to keep them in tune. As soon as they finish tuning those thousands of pipes, they have to start all over again! The sound this organ produces could be compared to 25 brass bands.

Rudolph Wurlitzer was quick to realize the importance of Hope Jones' invention and by 1913, Jones' unit orchestra organ was in full-scale production at the Wurlitzer theatre organ plant near Buffalo. Both Mr. Jones and Mr. Wurlitzer were fussy about their installations and had extremely high standards of quality. Even in the heyday of the Wurlitzer when orders were pouring in from all over the world, they did not lower their production standards, and produced, on average, an organ a day. Although some people accused the Wurlitzer organ of sounding mushy, they could not criticize it from a technical or quality point of view. The Hope Jones' Organ Works of Elmira, New York was absorbed in 1910 by the Wurlitzer Company. Many say Jones was not treated well by the Wurlitzer Company but there are two sides to this story.

Mr. Farney Wurlitzer spoke with great kindness about Hope Jones. He said, however, that Mr. Jones became more and more eccentric and more and more involved with each and every theatre organ installation to the point that he could not finish contracts. Jones would not release an organ until he was absolutely satisfied that it was perfect, and it seemed he never found it to be perfect. As a result, there was a falling out between Jones and Wurlitzer. Farney Wurlitzer told a wonderful story to Ed MacCormick and Bernie Venus of Toronto about one of his earliest installations in St. Paul's Church in Buffalo, New York. Wurlitzer had given the organ to the church but asked if, as a favour, he could use it from time to time to demonstrate the new theatre organ sound. In front of a group of theatre managers one night, the organist pulled out all the stops and the organ grew louder and louder until suddenly, at the most dramatic moment, the church's great stained glass window blew out into the street. Afterwards, the exhaust systems were changed so that no further explosions occurred. Sometimes when there was too much air pressure in pipe organs, smaller pipes took off like skyrockets from their bases and sailed into the air (another show-stopping finale).

Often the Wurlitzer console was raised on a lift high above the stage floor, nearly to the height of the balcony. Some consoles not only rose but could also pivot around so that

Organ consoles were sometimes mechanically raised by large worm gears which turned like giant screws lifting the organ to the desired position. When something went wrong with the mechanism, the results could be nothing short of electrifying.

Don Thompson. Organ consoles were nearly as elaborate as the theatres where they were installed. The "jelly mold" surrounding the keyboard lit up and changed colours in sync with the changing colours of the walls and ceiling of some theatres.

the organist faced the audience. Some rose hydraulically and some slid out of the wall instead of up out of the floor. But there were always a few that never descended properly. It was an organist's nightmare to have to be rescued by a rope and ladder because the organ could not be lowered. All the while the audience would be fuming, trying to see past the upright organ console and the great pole on which it sat. On at least one occasion, Toronto's Kathleen Stokes had to be rescued when her organ console became stuck in the highest position. It was difficult to remain dignified and elegant while climbing down a hastily erected, steep ladder, especially while wearing a white satin gown. Her descent brought tremendous applause.

Don Thompson, a fine Toronto theatre organist, tells of one terrifying occasion, which sounds rather amusing now. An organist pushed the descend button but nothing happened. He quickly pressed the ascend button, thinking that perhaps the organ was not fully in the "up" position. However, in his panic, he had actually pressed both buttons. To his horror, the organ kept rising until there were great flashes of fire as the electrical connections to the console were severed. Sparks flew out and the organ came to a wheezing, groaning stop, sounding like some beast in its death throes. But then the organ again started rising higher and higher, until finally it disengaged itself from its worm gear mechanism. It came right out of the housing which held it and, with the organist clutching the console, crashed through the movie screen! Talk about a theatrical exit.

Thompson, who has played in Canada, the United States and England, tells another marvellous story which took place in the Odeon Leicester Square in London, England. It seems that Queen Mary was very much addicted to the theatre organ and whenever she slipped quietly into the auditorium during an afternoon performance, the organist would be summoned to play her

The great console at the beautiful Odeon Leicester Square, London, England sports a "jelly mold" which changes colours to suit the musical mood.

Built in 1910 as a vaudeville theatre, Shea's Victoria had an unusually large number of ornate boxes (24). Although they were useless for movie viewers, they were ideal for watching live productions because of their closeness to the stage. The boxes were fitted with movable cane back chairs.

favourite piece, "Silver Threads Among the Gold," during the intermission. One day, however, she arrived when the organist was on vacation. A call was sent for a relief organist, but the regular relief organist was at a theatre quite far away from Leicester Square. He was told that Queen Mary was present in the audience and asked if he would get there as fast as possible. He dashed madly over by taxi, rushed into the theatre and to his horror noticed that the auditorium lights were on, and that the great house curtain had closed. He was probably too late! He dashed down the aisle and when he arrived at the orchestra pit there was no organ to be seen. Was he in the right theatre? What he did not know was that the organ console was in the "parking" position and was hidden beneath the orchestra platform. Seeing neither organ nor orchestra, he panicked and decided he was in the wrong theatre after all and that it must be the theatre across the square. He dashed frantically across the park, crashed past the doorman, rushed down to the theatre organist who was in the middle of playing, and, in clear view of the audience, shoved him to the floor! Meanwhile, Queen Mary was still waiting for "Silver Threads Among the Gold" at the theatre he had just left.

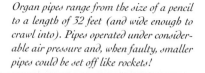

Organ pipes range from the size of a pencil to a length of 32 feet (and wide enough to crawl into). Pipes operated under considerable air pressure and, when faulty, smaller pipes could be set off like rockets!

Some theatre organists built up huge followings and many travelled all over the world playing to enormous crowds. Organists sang and led community singsongs and were themselves feature entertainers. One of the most famous, Mrs. Helen Crawford, had all her gowns designed with the decoration on the back because that was the audience view. Her husband, Jesse, was perhaps the best known of all American theatre organists. He became famous playing at the Chicago Theatre. After he was married, he had a special twin organ console built on the other side of the stage so that he and his wife could play at the same time. This act became enormously popular. They were so successful that when the famous Paramount Theatre opened in New York City, Jesse Crawford was given the opportunity to design the

The mightiest of Wurlitzers in the greatest of theatres — the organ at Radio City Music Hall, New York. This behemoth has a slave organ console so that more than one person can play it at the same time.

theatre organ to his own specifications. The result is considered by many enthusiasts to be the best theatre organ ever built.

Many fine theatre organs suffered badly through poor installations. Theatre owners and managers and circuit operators did not understand that by putting pipes underneath the stage, in the dome of the theatre, or perhaps behind certain architectural partitions, their sound was seriously distorted or diminished. Many architects believed that the organ grille, which was usually located above the box seats or in the area where a box seat would be, was unsightly and old-fashioned and they tried to hide it. As a result, the sound was often lost. Most organ pipes were located in two or three places: above the box seats on either side of the proscenium arch; in the proscenium arch itself; and just beneath the apron of the stage so that the sound would come from the same area as the orchestra. Some theatres also had pipes located in the dome of the theatre (sometimes referred to as the "echo organ").

Perhaps the most disastrous of all big theatre organ installations was in the great Roxy in New York. Most of its big pipes and its best voices were hidden underneath the stage so that when the enormous symphony orchestra was in position, the organ pipes sounded as if they were in the Bronx. There were several poor installations in England, too, where the "delay" —

between the moment the organist depressed the key until he could hear the sound—was so great that the organist could barely function.

Sometimes, when an organist pressed a key, the time it took for the air to rush through the pipe—which might be located 80 feet over his head—and then come back down through the auditorium was long enough for him to have finished playing the piece. It was sometimes easier to wear ear plugs because if the organist was playing a rapid number it was extremely confusing not to hear what he was playing but, in fact, what he had already played! This led to many jokes about delays in theatre organs. One such joke was that the delay was so great in one London theatre that the audience was standing at attention listening to the last few bars of "God Save the King" while the organist was on his way home.

In England, theatre organs were installed and theatre organists trained long after organs had ceased to be used in the United States. When sound movies came to the United States, almost overnight nearly all the organists were fired except for a few in certain enormous theatres. This did not happen in England because if the theatre organ was played, the theatre enjoyed a tax exemption because the organist was considered "live" entertainment. In England, organists played during

The Wurlitzer organ at Vancouver's Orpheum.

Quentin McLean, Shea's Hippodrome's most famous organist, arrived in Toronto from England and stayed on for eight years!

the intermission long after sound films came in, even until after the Second World War.

Organists played at supper shows and at children's matinees, where the occasional apple bounced off their heads. Many organists inspired rather fanatical fan clubs. The theatre organ achieved a greater amount of respectability in England than it ever did in the United States. It was, however, a sad day when the tax exemption was rescinded and the great Odeon circuit fired nearly all of its organists. The organs were not removed, however, and on special occasions they are still played. Throughout England, many usable theatre organs are still maintained in excellent condition. Very few remain in theatres in the United States. There is only one in Canada, at the Orpheum in Vancouver, which is no longer a theatre but a concert hall.

At different times, all three English organists played the Wurlitzer at London's Trocadero Theatre. Mr. Torch considered the organ there to be very challenging because it was only partly unified, unlike most theatre organs. The Trocadero advertised it as "The Wizard Organ." It cost 15,000 pounds, weighed 15 tons and had a sound to match.

The Roxy organ of New York had a mammoth white and antique gold console with five keyboards flanked by two equally ornate consoles of three keyboards each. All three rose out of the depths together and were an eye-popping spectacle!

But the sound was not equal to the sight. The size, weight, cost, the number of consoles were not really the crucial factors in the sound of an organ. The installation was critical and the Roxy organ suffered from a poor installation.

Among the great organists of England were Quentin McLean (who later came to Canada and played at Shea's Hippodrome and is perhaps Canada's best known theatre organist); Sydney Torch, who played at London's Odeon Regal (later the Odeon Marble Arch); and Reginald Foort. Quentin McLean was already famous when he came to Toronto to play as a guest organist for six weeks. By popular demand, he stayed for eight years. On several occasions after solo performances, he received standing ovations from appreciative audiences.

Don Baker, Canada's only internationally-known theatre organist, was at the Brooklyn Paramount after Jesse Crawford and played the Paramount during the big band era. He was born in St. Thomas, Ontario, then moved to Calgary. From there he went to New York and got a job as a relief organist at the Rivoli theatre.

Kathleen Stokes, "The Grand Lady of the Canadian Theatre Organ," and later member of the American Theatre Organists' Hall of Fame, was a star in Toronto theatres for over fifty years. After 1937, when theatre organists were to a

The great Sydney Torch, one of England's most famous organists, at Britain's biggest console (complete with "jelly mold").

Casa Loma

large extent unemployed, Kathleen was plucked from the keyboard at Shea's Hippodrome and given a job with the CBC's national radio show "The Happy Gang." This became one of the most popular radio shows ever. Running for 22 years and 4,890 broadcasts, the show made Kay Stokes, playing the Hammond organ, one of Canada's best known personalities.

Stokes was born in 1894 in Durham, Ontario, and by age nine was playing the organ for church services in St. Catharines. Her first big job was playing at the Astor Theatre in Toronto (now the New Yorker) for $12 a week. Kay played almost all of the big theatres in Toronto, including the Loew's Uptown and Loew's Yonge Street, which was her favourite.

Not all theatre organists played in theatres. In fact, many theatre organs were not installed in theatres at all but in big convention halls and hotel ballrooms. After many of the great movie palaces disappeared, theatre organs were often salvaged and rebuilt in new places such as Toronto's Casa Loma. Casa Loma is a fairyland castle built by an eccentric millionaire in 1913. It has all the escapist architecture of an old movie palace. Its organ has been lovingly restored by Bernie Venus and a group of dedicated technicians. Izz Gang, a great theatre organ enthusiast, has for several years been the very capable master of ceremonies at the monthly organ concerts.

Venus also has his own private Wurlitzer from the Granada Theatre in Buffalo. It looks and sounds marvellous right in his Toronto home. The sound is never overpowering because it enters the room through a fairly small opening from an underground room where the pipes are located. The sound filters through shutters hidden behind large wooden Chinese characters.

Another unusual installation is in the home of Roy Bingham in Derbyshire, England. Roy lives in a magnificently-restored thatched cottage near a castle. Upstairs, beneath the thatched roof, is a beautiful Wurlitzer organ complete with all the sound effects for which the mighty Wurlitzer was famous. Roy also has this organ equipped so that it will sound like a straight concert organ. For many years he was the organist at the Elite Theatre in Nottingham and he has made many recordings in England. This organ has a lovely sound because the pipes are located next to a large family room on the top floor. The sound comes into the room through small, controlled apertures.

There are many theatre organs throughout the United States and in parts of Canada, Australia, New Zealand and South Africa which have been installed in theatre restaurants, high school auditoriums, universities, convention halls and even department stores. The organ from the Odeon Carlton in Toronto was given to Queen's University in Kingston. Theatre organ enthusiasts are very active and through the efforts of their unorthodox "midnight organ supply company," many organs sound better, look better and are better maintained than they ever were before. The "Mighty Wurlitzer" plays on.

The Odeon Toronto, later the Odeon Carlton, on opening night in 1948. The "Showplace of the Dominion" was the flagship of Canadian Odeon Theatres. The huge British Odeon theatre circuit made inroads into Canada after the Second World War but could not penetrate the United States market. In 1978, with 250 screens and 168 theatres, it became a wholly-owned Canadian company. Later it became the backbone of Cineplex Odeon, which was also Canadian. This fantastic movie palace (now gone) was the largest theatre of its type ever built in North America.

5 THE CIRCUITS

"IMMEDIATE SEATING ON ALL FLOORS, PLEASE WAIT IN THE GRAND FOYER!" is a sign seldom seen today. Yet it once stood in scores of big movie palaces, owned by huge theatre circuits, all over North America. Where are those big circuits and big theatres now? Odeon, Allen's, Balaban & Katz, Loew's, Famous Players, R.K.O., Fox, Paramount, Publix, Warner's, United Artists and the others? What happened to Bennett's, B.F. Keith, Stair and Havlin, Orpheum, Pantages, Shea's and other vaudeville circuits?

Ruthless competition has always dominated show business. The ethics of theatre circuit operators often leave much to be desired. This is as true in the new millennium as it was at the turn of the twentieth century. Canada's Bennett circuit faced one of the earliest struggles. It was formed in London, Ontario near the turn of the century. The backers included Mr. Smallman, of the Smallman and Ingraham department store, and, of course, Mr. Bennett, who was the successful

Bennett's Theatre, Montreal

*The Bennett circuit's Majestic Theatre,
London, Ontario*

owner-operator of the elegant Bennett's Theatre in London.
The circuit owned and operated theatres in Hamilton, Ottawa,
St. Thomas, Montreal, Quebec City, Halifax and Sydney.

The Bennett Theatre in Quebec, one of their finest theatres,
was close to the port at Wolfe's Cove where the great liners
arrived from England and Europe. Its great, long entrance
way, oval-shaped lobby and split staircase complete with
stained glass windows retains its elegance even today. This
theatre, later called the Capitol, showed movies until it was
restored thanks to support from the government of Quebec.
Originally opened in 1903 and prominently located in the
Place D'Youville, it was modestly called "The Auditorium."
In 1927, Thomas Lamb remodelled it extensively and in
1992, it became a live venue.

The American circuits sent shows to their own big-time vaudeville theatres. When they lost a few customers to the Bennett vaudeville theatres "up there in Canada," they were not overly concerned. That would change when the Bennett circuit expanded operations and eventually built a series of Bijou movie theatres across the country. The playbill from the 1907-1908 season at the Bennett's Theatre in Hamilton advertised, "The Bennettograph—Moving Pictures of Interest and Comedy." This clearly shows the vision the Bennett circuit showed in the development of the movies, an interest

The Savoy Hamilton was the earliest of the city's four large theatres. It opened c.1907 as a Bennett vaudeville theatre bringing top shows direct from New York.

that was later to doom it. The same playbill states that the Bennetts were affiliated with Percy William's Orpheum Theatre in New York and also with Hammerstein's Victoria Theatre, and Hammerstein's Paradise Roof Garden in New York. It was a Canadian circuit with big connections. There were even plans to expand into the South American market. These plans were too much for the rival circuits who began systematically to cut off many of the best acts and famous performers. It is likely that rivals waited until the Bennett circuit was overextended before taking action. By about 1910, all of the Bennett theatres were sold to rivals and the Bennett empire was finished.

The Bijou Theatre, St. Stephen, N. B.

The name Bijou was favoured by the Bennett circuit when it began to collect nickelodeons and to convert a few of its smaller vaudeville houses to movies. This New Brunswick Bijou was typical of the era.

Much later came the "unit shows" once movies had become more important than vaudeville. Packaged in New York or California, unit shows, such as those by Fanchon & Marco, were meant to travel to theatres in a circuit which presented shows designed especially for that circuit. These unit shows made it possible for theatres in relatively small cities to put on far more spectacular shows than local talent budgets could provide. These shows were highly successful even in the biggest theatres in the largest cities. As the unit shows moved in, many local performers, like organist Horace Lapp of Toronto, were pushed out of theatre after theatre.

St. Catherine Street. East. MONTREAL. Rue Ste. Catherine Est

This turn-of-the-century post card shows the independent Théâtre Français on St. Catherine Street, Montreal.

There were two favourite methods used to destroy the competition. The quickest way was to cut off the product and then move in when the circuit ratings began to slip. The other method was to lease land across the street from a competitor's theatre and put up a huge sign announcing plans to build a new multi-million dollar theatre on the site. It was not even necessary to begin to build the theatre to achieve the desired result. Often the competitor would sell rather than face the competition a big new theatre would offer.

There was big money to be made running a vaudeville circuit. In 1912, the E.D. Stair and Havlin vaudeville circuit in the United States was reputed to be worth $15 million. B.F. Keith, another big vaudeville circuit owner, made a $5 million fortune

This later view of theatre row on St. Catherine St. shows how the circuits had taken over.

Garbo in The Painted Veil, *1954. Garbo was among the plethora of stars belonging to Hollywood's biggest studio, MGM (the production arm of Loew's Inc.) The MGM/Loew's connection was the basis of the "studio system" in which production, distribution and exhibition were all controlled.*

while Marcus Loew had to be content with a trifling $1.5 million. Loew, however, went on to become the richest of them all. When Marcus Loew died in 1924, his estate was worth over $50 million. In 1923, the Mayer Company and Metro Pictures were sold to Loew and by 1924 Metro Goldwyn Mayer was formed. Owned by the parent company, Loew's Theatres Inc., its president was Loew's own Nicholas Schenck. Irving Thalberg was Supervisor of Production. The company was formed from two earlier movie companies, Metro Pictures (formed in 1915) and the Mayer Company run by Louis B. Mayer, the biggest movie mogul of them all. L.B. Mayer was from Saint John, New Brunswick.

Powerful movie production companies such as MGM later showed their movies in their own theatres, operating very much like the old vaudeville circuits. Circuits like Loew's (MGM) made their money using ruthless business tactics so that many small operators, like the Bennetts, were pushed out of business.

Theatre circuit mogul, Alexander Pantages, operated many theatres in Canada and the U.S. Later, due to cutthroat competition, his circuit was largely confined to the West.

One of the most ruthless businessmen was Alexander Pantages, whose very difficult early life perhaps accounted for his attitude. He was born in Greece but at the age of seven hopped on a freighter and sailed away. He ended up some years later in America after a long journey via South America. Working his way to a new life on a broken down ship must have prepared him for anything. In his mid-twenties, he joined the great Klondike Gold Rush in 1897. When he lost his last thousand dollars gambling, he became a waiter to make some quick money. While waiting on tables he met and became very involved with Kate Rockwell, a former Coney Island chorus girl. Kate Rockwell, known as "Klondike Kate" and "The Belle

Its name, the Palace Grande, was impressive, but its architecture left much to be desired. Even the gold miners got into the act when they dropped their mining gear and dressed in drag. This was the kind of show that inspired Pantages to enter the theatre business during his stay in Dawson City.

of the Yukon" became a legendary figure inspiring scores of stories. She made thousands of dollars each month singing and dancing (among other things). Legend has it that Pantages became a pimp for Kate during those crazy days of the gold rush.

Although Pantages knew next to nothing about show business, he persuaded Kate to invest a good chunk of her money in a theatre that he and a few of his friends wanted to open. The Orpheum in Dawson City became a popular spot with the sourdoughs. Alexander Pantages himself could often be seen sweeping up after the performance. Why? Because he had noticed drunken miners spilling gold dust on the floor. He eventually ran off with a great deal of poor Kate's money and skipped off to Seattle where he operated a theatre.

A devious operator, Pantages was known to steal actors' trunks from the train station and take them to his theatre! When the worried actor arrived to claim his baggage at Pantages' theatre he was usually very relieved to find it had not been stolen, only taken to the wrong theatre by mistake. An apologetic Alexander Pantages would then convince the actor that he would be better off performing at Pantages' establishment, thus stealing the actor away from a rival theatre.

Business was very good in the early days of the West, especially during the gold rush. Miners paid enormous sums of money to escape the bleak reality of the frontier. Pantages knew this, bankrolled his idea and turned it into the great Pantages Vaudeville Circuit. Eventually the Hollywood Pantages became its flagship.

Perhaps the toughest of all the circuits in America was the T.O.B.A. Circuit. It was for black vaudeville performers only. In the days when the colour bar was in force, T.O.B.A. theatres were the only theatres that welcomed black actors and musicians. The key theatre in the circuit was the Lyric in New Orleans. Great performers and American Jazz came out of this theatre and the circuit. Some indication of just how tough things were playing the T.O.B.A.

The Bennett vaudeville theatre in Ottawa has long since been razed. Vaudeville was big business. Vaudeville mogul B.F. Keith (of New York Palace fame) was worth over five million dollars in 1912.

The Allen name lights up the Palace marquee in Calgary.

circuit can best be understood when, for many performers, the letters "T.O.B.A.," stood for "Tough on Black Asses."

Many great stars of this circuit made the transition to big time vaudeville and played the New York Palace. The T.O.B.A. Circuit, with its collection of cramped, poorly equipped theatres, made a tough school for performers in the early stages of their careers. The T.O.B.A. Circuit of theatres did not exist in Canada.

The first big international movie theatre circuit was Canadian. It began in Brantford, Ontario in 1906, backed by the Allen family, and spread to every minor city in Canada and included cities in the northeastern United States. It was a giant long before United Artists was founded in 1919. A 1920 advertisement for Allen enterprises in the Toronto newspaper *Mail & Empire*, describes the Allen empire:

> *With many theatres in Canada as yet in the early construction stages or taking form in the architectural department, the Allen theatre enterprises already have invaded the amusement field in the United States and Great Britain. In this respect the Allen theatre enterprises are unique in the amusement field, extending their theatres, methods, and Canadian influence into more countries than other concerns connected with motion pictures.*

The Allen chain consisted of over fifty theatres in Canada, seven in Toronto alone. All of the Toronto theatres had seating capacities of over 1,500. The Calgary Allen (1913) has been acclaimed as Canada's first "deluxe" movie theatre. Even though it had only about 900 seats, it still boasted a theatre organ.

The large, iron, vertical sign and marquee light up Cleveland's Playhouse Square. The cost of building this theatre helped to bankrupt the Allen Circuit.

The Allen Palace in Montreal, one of Canada's largest and most elaborate vaudeville/movie palaces, was designed by C. Howard Crane who did many theatres for the Allens, but whose greatest achievement was the famous Detroit Fox. The Allen Palace held nearly 3,000 and was an especially elaborate theatre for 1921. It was noted for its magnificent frieze and elaborate side walls, which featured enormous arched windows towering above the exits. The multi-paned, fabric-backed windows were back-lit to provide atmospheric lighting. They were beautifully draped and rose above ornate balconies. Carved plaster ornamentation crowned the arches over the exits making them look like entrances to a palace rather than fire exits.

The Canadian Allen Circuit gained a foothold in the United States with the beautiful Allen in Cleveland but failed to further penetrate the American market.

The name "palace" was not a misnomer. The wonderfully restored Allen in Cleveland, Ohio, part of that city's Playhouse Square theatre complex, has an auditorium, slightly more restrained but otherwise very similar. However, the Cleveland Allen, also a Crane design, has a lobby and entrance far more grand than the Allen in Montreal ever had.

Unfortunately, although there were plans to build new theatres and take over existing ones in England and Russia, disaster struck the Allen circuit shortly after the opening of the Cleveland Allen. While Mr. Allen was vacationing in Hawaii, he received a dramatic telegram stating that, because his theatre empire had overextended itself, and because of the difficulty in obtaining new movies for the circuit (thanks to the blocking efforts of Paramount Pictures in New York), Allen theatres were left with insufficient product and with a staggering bank loan. In the end, Allen lost the entire circuit and Allen theatre enterprises, "the masterpiece in plays and playhouses," became a thing of the past.

The Allen theatre circuit was replaced by Famous Players of Canada Ltd. in 1916. When Allen still reigned supreme, this fledgling outfit purchased one theatre, the dingy old Majestic in Toronto. The 1,175-seat theatre was renamed The Regent and was renovated and greatly improved by Thomas Lamb, who also designed the Capitol in Brantford for the

The early marque of Toronto's Hollywood Theatre.

The Metropolitan's comfortable lobby at the mezzanine level led directly to the select "dress circle" section of the balcony.

ALLEN THEATRE-WINNIPEG.
NO.71. MEYERS PHOTO JAN. 2ND 1920

Allens. This "Canadian" chain, founded by Nathan Nathanson and financed by E.L. Ruddy, the billboard advertising king, was soon controlled by American interests. "Ruddy" signs accounted for Famous Players' rather grand, and frequently changed marquees. Later, when Ruddy's interest in Famous Players was withdrawn, the marquees became smaller and uglier with each "modernization." The final insult to grand marquees were dinky

The attractive auditorium of "The Met" (as it was affectionately called) was more typical of a legitimate theatre than of a vaudeville/movie house. Note the curved backstage wall. This unusual "bandshell" stage configuration was designed to reflect music back to the audience. The black curtain above the orchestra is covering the small, vertical format, movie screen.

185

In the days when flashing lights and grand marquees drew in the crowds, the Hamilton Capitol was in the forefront.

plastic signs above cheap canvas awnings like the one at the Hollywood Theatre in Toronto. By the year 2000 much grander signage would appear on many of the megaplexes such as Famous Player's "Paramount" in Toronto, or Cineplex Odeon's "Grande" theatres there.

In the early years, after being bought up by Paramount, the Hollywood production company, Famous Players was not interested in supporting the Canadian motion picture industry which had just begun in Trenton, Ontario. Because of the lack of support, and because Canadian motion pictures had difficulty finding theatres to show them, the Canadian motion picture industry all but collapsed. The Regent, which for a while was Toronto's premiere Famous Players house, did show a few Canadian movies. In November 1920, The *Star* newspaper carried an advertisement for a Canadian movie showing at the Regent, *Carry on Sergeant*. Despite its hardships, the Canadian film industry managed to create innovative technical advances. Canadians were the first to experiment with colour on North American screens and the first to use sound in their movies. Some daring investors like Sir Henry Pellat, who

The Capitol, North Bay (which has been saved) had a marquee which would not have been out of place in any big city.

built the world famous Casa Loma in Toronto, lost a bundle on movies. He invested in a colour film process called chromacolour. It was apparently very good, perhaps too good for the competition. It was shown quite regularly in theatres across the country in a series of film shorts. The American movie companies had their own process and they were not pleased to have a rival. The message was sent out to the movie theatre exhibitors: "If you show chromacolour shorts in your theatres we will not send you our full length feature films." It was not long before Sir Henry lost his investment and the chromacolour company went out of business.

Famous Players' Regent Theatre was soon followed by many others and by 1920, with capital of $15 million, including a $4 million loan from Lord Beaverbrook, the chain was well on its way to becoming Canada's largest. The crowning achievement came when the chain obtained the Toronto Pantages. Apparently, Nathanson was instrumental in financing the construction of this theatre as far back as 1919 because his vision was to some day have it as his flagship. This finally happened in

The Victoria, B.C. Pantages has been restored and renamed the McPhearson Playhouse.

1930 after vaudeville had waned and the Pantages circuit was in decline. The Pantages' 3,626 seats and 22,500 square feet made it the second largest theatre after the Capitol in New York. The New York Capitol was built by the same architect, Thomas Lamb, in the same Adam and Empire style. On March 15, 1930, the Pantages became the Imperial and was the flagship of Famous Players until it was hacked to pieces to become the Imperial Six. However, this was not the end of the Pantages. The Imperial Six closed in 1987 only to undergo another transformation; this time, a wonderful one. Through the efforts of Garth Drabinsky and the Livent company, not to mention some $18 million, the Pantages was reborn. Opening night crowds who came to see *The Phantom of the Opera* on September 20, 1989 were dazzled by the opulence of the place.

In 1931, Famous Players was charged under the Canadian Combines Investigations Act. It was felt to be too big and too American. The case was dismissed by an Ontario court and the company did not alter its operations. Famous Players was (and still is) Canada's largest circuit. Even in the 1970s, it had 4,000 employees in cinemas across Canada. It now controls over 450 screens in about 250 theatres and millions of Canadians attend Famous Players theatres every year. (As early as the 1940s, Famous Players advertised the fact that 35 million people attended their theatres.)

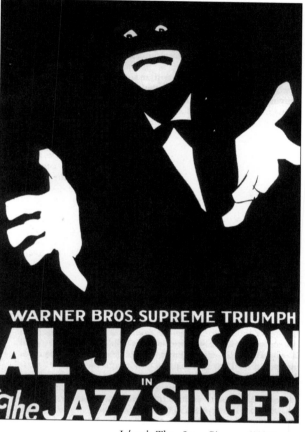

WARNER BROS. SUPREME TRIUMPH
AL JOLSON
IN
The JAZZ SINGER

Jolson's The Jazz Singer *(1927) was the first feature to contain speech. "Talkies" brought a boom to the cinema. In the U.S., weekly attendance rose from 60 million in 1927 to 90 million in 1930.*

The marquee of the Loew's London Theatre. Similar marquees sprouted up all over North America as Loew's huge chain switched from featuring small-time vaudeville to playing Metro-Goldwyn-Mayer pictures.

Until quite recently, Famous Players was 51 percent Canadian-owned but that is no longer true. When Famous Players was busy tearing down their theatres in the hearts of cities during the 1980s, they were motivated by the fact that even the theatres themselves were owned by an American real estate company which was entirely separate from Famous Players and its parent company, Gulf and Western/Viacom. In the case of Toronto's University Theatre, the exhibition arm of Famous Players wanted to save it, while the real estate arm wanted to sell the property. Guess who won?

Early in the development of the movie industry in the United States, production companies and theatre circuits merged and formed enormous monopolies. This had a dramatic effect on independent theatre operators and movie producers because it soon became apparent that it was very hard to do business if one did not have a chain affiliated directly with a movie production company, or vice versa. One of the biggest monopolies was Loew's, which began producing movies in 1919 in order to protect its vast theatre holdings from rival motion picture circuits. Anti-trust laws in the United

States broke these chains and destroyed the monopolies. This did not happen in Canada.

Canadian Louis B. Mayer, who lived in Saint John, New Brunswick, made his living in the rag trade, a humble beginning for a motion picture pioneer who was to become a movie mogul. But Mayer did not forget his friends in Saint John. This is why the Imperial Theatre, which opened there in 1913, was quite grand. It was designed by a famous architect from Philadelphia, and had all the elegance and style of theatres in Philadelphia and in New York. The Imperial's manager, Walter Gilding, was a life-long friend of Mayer's.

Likely through Mayer's influence, the Imperial Theatre took on grand proportions and attracted some big names like Sir Harry Lauder, Ethel Barrymore, Sir John Martin Harvey, Burns and Allen, and Gracie Fields. Walter Pidgeon, also from Saint John, made several appearances. The Imperial Theatre,

Canadian Louis B. Mayer once lived in Saint John, N.B. and made a living in the rag trade—a humble beginning for the biggest movie mogul of them all.

The Imperial Theatre in St. John N.B., built in 1913, is a highlight in the ongoing struggle to save Canada's theatres. This grand old theatre has been beautifully restored inside and out.

The beautifully decorated auditorium of the Imperial Theatre, St. John, N.B.

The Imperial was restored by Hannivan and Company, theatre restoration experts specializing in painting and gilding.

after a stunning $11.3 million renovation, still enjoys its attractive setting on King Square in Saint John. (Louis B. Mayer would probably have enjoyed the story that the great Metro-Goldwyn-Mayer Company at one time came very close to being Metro Goldfish and Mayer. Those in charge rightly thought that a name change would sound much better.)

The Odeon circuit made a tremendous impact in 1948 when it opened the Odeon Toronto, "The Showplace Of The Dominion." Although it was the period when sound was in and regular live shows were out, this theatre, built especially with sound in mind, had many of the trappings of the movie palace era. This new "moderne" movie palace had a klieg-lit opening on Carlton Street complete with guest stars on its great stage, guest theatre organist Al Bolington, flags galore, crowds of people and the premiere of a British picture.

Full use was made of its three lobbies and theatre restaurant, although Ontario's archaic liquor laws kept the bar closed. In the auditorium, hundreds of hidden lights constantly changed colours on the smooth plastered walls. This frequently changing light and colour was accomplished through a patented lighting panel called a

The curtain at the Odeon Toronto was reputed to weigh nearly 2 1/2 tons. Each swag of drapery was lifted by a separate motor. (Note the theatre organ to the right.)

"Thyratron, painting with light." The enormous two and a half ton contour (sculpted) curtain rose slowly, its various motors lifting each swag to a predetermined height. The curtain also changed colour to match the changing colour of the walls of the big auditorium. The smooth line of the balcony swept around in a great gentle curve flaring out at the side walls to accommodate large aisles. The auditorium held 2,300 richly upholstered seats, although it was spacious enough for 3,000 or more, and every inch of the floor was broadloomed. The woodwork was light blonde and the mural on the grand staircase was in pastel tones depicting the theme of motion picture making. The trim was stainless steel with huge areas of mirror and other glass.

The Ziegfeld Follies *was originally a much-loved live show. This 1946 film was shot on* Technicolor, *a colour process invented by Professor Herbert Kalmus, a Canadian from Queen's University.*

The Odeon Toronto's marquee with its huge vertical sign was the biggest Toronto had ever seen before or since.

The Odeon Toronto was certainly Canada's most spectacular post Second World War movie theatre, but Canada's big "Super Cinema," its "Picture Palace," was not to last. One sad and cold night in 1974, only a handful of people came to the theatre to see Burt Reynolds in *White Lightning*, among the few who knew it was the last night the great marquee would light up Carlton Street. The organist, Colin Corbett, played an emotional farewell and when he descended, people supposedly ran up the aisles onto the stage demanding to hear more. The credits for *White Lightning*

Note the sunburst design on the Stanley's marquee, Vancouver. Pulsating sun rays were a favourite effect used with light bulbs in the days before neon. When the theatre opened in December of 1930, it screened Lillian Gish's first talkie, One Romantic Night.

The Stanley was built by Frederick Guest, the owner of a theatre chain in southern Ontario. He used Tyndall stone from Winnipeg on the exterior—the same stone used to build the Parliament Buildings in Ottawa.

were doused from the big screen and the organ came up again. There was more applause and a few tears until down it went forever. A sullen group stood around on the cold sidewalk out front, stamping their feet, waiting to see the lights go out for the last time on the giant marquee. The CBC TV cameras were there to record the event—and that was it.

A few weeks later, the City of Toronto was given the opportunity to buy the place for one dollar to use as a theatre, perhaps for the National Ballet or the Canadian Opera Company. There was a silly hassle over a few feet of land needed to deepen the stage and the city administrators noted that the O'Keefe Centre for the Performing Arts with 3,200 seats built in the early '60s was losing money anyway—so down it came.

Well-built and constructed mainly of concrete, the Odeon took months to destroy, and bankrupted the wrecking company. There were those who had felt the Odeon was cold, sterile and barn-like. They said it was too Art Deco and looked as if it belonged to the HMS Queen Mary. The building, designed for the Rank Organisation, was very close to the plan used by Harry W. Weedon in his Odeons of England. London's world-renowned Odeon Leicester Square was smaller but otherwise very similar to the Odeon Toronto, except for a more fanciful treatment of its side walls. At least the Art Deco style was come by honestly. The thing that is really surprising is that it was built with a full stage and a theatre organ as late as 1948!

There were other modern theatres built after the Odeon Toronto, many of them by the Odeon circuit. Famous Players did not remain idle either. Famous Players' University on Bloor Street in Toronto was one. On the inside it resembled a smaller version of the Esquire Theatre in Chicago, built in the late 1930s. The

It took six years of effort and millions of dollars to restore the Stanley after it was shut down by Famous Players in 1991.

197

Trimmed with pulsating neon, this giant "Imperial" sign was one of Famous Players' largest. The Imperial Toronto was formerly the Pantages.

University (c.1949) was designed by Eric W. Hounsom and was most notable for its lovely curved façade with an enormous two-and-a-half storey window overlooking Toronto's fashionable Bloor Street. The theatre suffered some drastic renovations to accommodate a new wide screen. Its original screen, installed just before television spurred wider ones, was almost as tall as it was wide. (Most early movie screens were actually taller than they were wide.)

In many of the old movie palaces, the advent of the new wider screen was accommodated without much difficulty. The screen stretched across the entire width of the proscenium arch anyway but was very high, so the top was masked off. In the case of the Toronto's Imperial theatre, it was cut down by almost half. The curtains were then put on a slower motor so they seemed to take for ever to open, giving the effect of great width. To install the wide screen, especially for 70mm at the University, required that the theatre auditorium be changed. A new screen was installed with its own curtains on a new stage projecting many rows out into the auditorium. This spoiled the sight lines of the original but did make for a much wider screen. It did not help the decoration of the original interior. The super-wide screens resulted in the destruction of original stages and parts of the interiors of many North American movie palaces.

Joan of Arc lights up Toronto's University Theatre marquee. Over 25,000 people signed a petition to save this theatre (as well as the Eglinton Theatre) but to no avail.

The Eglinton was designed by Kaplan and Sprachman in 1936. This lovely neighbourhood theatre which seats only about 800 seems enormous today. Sprachman's son Mandel is one of Canada's leading theatre architects.

When Famous Players decided to replace the University Theatre—the last large movie theatre with a single auditorium left in downtown Toronto —with a new one on the same site with "perhaps more than one auditorium," over 25,000 people signed a petition to save it. They also signed to save the venerable Eglinton, a lovely neighbourhood Art Deco theatre dating back to the 1930s. The Eglinton was listed by the City of Toronto as a heritage building and is still going strong, but the University, except for its façade which was deemed worthy of architectural merit, has been a parking lot for years.   The Eglinton's beautiful vertical sign and period marquee are a delight to see on Eglinton Avenue. Designed by Sprachman and Kaplan, its authentic Art Deco auditorium, complete with a recessed neon ceiling and tacky statues over the exits (two naked women with their arms flung up) has been voted as Toronto's favourite movie theatre as late as 1998. The Eglinton's screen is quite enormous when compared to those in the multiplexes that later sprang up like weeds.

The step from Art Deco and the "Cinema Moderne" to multiplex cinemas in Canada was taken swiftly, so swiftly in fact, that few people even noticed. The first significant shot to destroy grand movie palaces was fired in Toronto when Garth Drabinsky and Nat Taylor opened 18 tiny cinemas with small screens and sound to match in a converted Eaton Centre parking garage. This eventually led to much better multiplexes under their Cineplex Odeon banner. Drabinsky did have a vision to build a new kind of movie palace where movie-going would once more become an event, but he was ousted from his position as head of Cineplex Odeon before it could be fully realized.

Today's movie theatres seem to have come full circle. The grand movie palace of 2,000-3,000 seats has been replaced by small auditoriums in megaplex theatres that are reminiscent of the penny arcades and nickelodeons of the beginning of the twentieth century. Throughout, the basic formula for attracting audiences to the movies has remained the same—making theatre-going an event in itself. As Joseph Valerio and Daniel Friedman observe in *Movie Palaces: Renaissance and the Reuse*, movies and movie palaces "transform worlds, providing the patron with a sense of removal from the commonplace." Penny arcades and nickelodeons achieved this by wowing audiences with their marvelous hand-cranked, card-flipping machines; grand movie palaces inspired patrons with their size and elegance; and today's stadium-type theatres provide spectacle with giant neon-lit lobbies crammed with espresso machines, video games and fast food stands. The new megaplex is a vast improvement over the earlier multiplexes, but few have architectural merit. Sight lines are better than ever before, screens are bigger, sound is superior, and the seats are more

The cove-lit neon ceiling and statues over the exits are some of the design features which give the Eglinton the feeling of a 1930s Hollywood movie set.

Shown here in its vaudeville days, the Vancouver Orpheum was the largest and finest theatre belonging to the Orpheum circuit in Canada.

The Orpheum, Winnipeg, (c.1910) had a giant vertical sign and featured a marquee with a "French curve."

comfortable, but still they are not movie palaces. Does one love a particular multiplex above all others?

Thankfully, not all of our theatres have been lost. By the late 1980s, there was a new appreciation of these theatres which was not present in the 60s and 70s. One of the first of several success stories was the saving of Vancouver's Orpheum Theatre. Many years ago when Famous Players bought what was left of the Orpheum circuit in Canada, one of its prizes was the beautiful Vancouver Orpheum. The theatre did very well for Famous Players for many years but when the era of multiplexing came in, they decided not to convert the Orpheum. Famous Players already owned the Capitol next door and decided to hack it up instead of the Orpheum. The Orpheum was then put up for sale.

When the Orpheum was threatened, Vancouver theatre-lovers sprang into action. Unlike the Ottawa Capitol, the Orpheum was reborn, bigger and grander than ever. The Mayor was deluged with 8,500 letters asking for the theatre's preservation. Lotteries were held and a special Jack Benny benefit was held in which private donations raised $400,000. The Vancouver Symphony Orchestra, the newly formed Community Arts Council and the Mayor were all influential in ensuring the restoration of the Orpheum. In 1975, the architects and engineers moved in and work began.

The symphony hall treatment of the stage was cleverly executed to blend with the original auditorium. The Orpheum has been a beloved fixture on Granville Street for decades.

One glorious night in 1927, Vancouverites flocked to Granville Street to see *The Wise Wife* at the opening of the new Orpheum. They were impressed with the opulence of the 2,788-seat theatre which replaced the 1914 Orpheum. They may not have been thrilled with the movie, or the stage show which featured *Toto the Clown* and the *Dance Delineators*, but they were thrilled by the theatre itself. There it was, with its 100

In 1949, The Orpheum in Vancouver sported newer and flashier signage to add pizazz to Vancouver's theatre row.

chandeliers, ornate columns, massive 60-foot diameter dome, ornate plaster work and magnificent proscenium arch, for all of Vancouver to admire.

Fifty years later, an entirely different generation of Vancouverites flocked to the same spot to see the opening of the new Orpheum and to hear the Vancouver Symphony Orchestra. Once again the main attraction was the theatre itself—and what they saw was very similar to that which was seen in 1927. Vancouverites were very impressed with the newly restored dome painted by Tony Heinsbergen. He was the 82-year-old decorator and painter who had worked on the original construction of the building. The canvasses were painted in Los Angeles and brought to Vancouver where the artist and two assistants spent more than two months, high on a 70-foot scaffolding, preparing the mural. In the centre of the dome is the original massive chandelier which can be lowered for rebulbing and cleaning. To allow for the new concert hall, the proscenium arch was raised somewhat and the ornate columns moved back to flank the enlarged stage floor. Molds were taken of the original columns from the side-wall treatment of the theatre and duplicated on the front of the sound shell. It was a very faithful restoration.

Vancouverites are proud of the fact that Charlie Chaplin and Bob Hope once played there, Igor Stravinsky conducted the symphony and Margot Fonteyn danced on its stage. They

Above: *Usherettes at the Vancouver Orpheum by day. Below: Usherettes in their evening attire. One of them was Juliette of CBC fame.*

Ivan Ackery and George Burns. Ackery, the colourful long-time manager of the Orpheum, once disrupted downtown traffic with 130 milk wagons and horses in order to plug the movie The Kid From Brooklyn *starring Danny Kaye.*

refer to the Orpheum as "the grand old lady of Granville Street." North American music critics have called the concert hall magnificent and "an acoustic delight." Vancouver's citizens gave their verdict on the grand old lady in her renewed finery—"you're not getting older, you're getting better." Now the great Wurlitzer organ is able to rise out of the stage to thrill the audiences once again. It is the only one in Canada in its original theatre setting.

The Orpheum is one of three very bright spots in the history of saving Canada's largest theatres. (Toronto's Pantages and Loew's/Winter Garden are the others.) Thankfully there are more success stories among our smaller theatres.

A great deal of the Orpheum Theatre's success was due to its long-time manager, Ivan Ackery. He has won more show business awards than anyone else in Canada, including the cherished Quigley Award which is bestowed on the most enterprising theatre managers for outstanding showmanship. It is the Academy Award of the motion picture exhibition business and is coveted by thousands of managers all over North America. Mr. Ackery has won it several times.

Ivan Ackery eased his way into show business many years ago as a singing usher in Vancouver's Capitol Theatre. He soon learned the tricks of the trade and, before long, rose to the position of Assistant Manager. He was then made Manager of the Victoria Road Theatre in suburban Vancouver. After a successful stay, he went to the Dominion (originally an Allen theatre built in 1907) and there began to develop his style as a promoter of films. Once during the showing of the film *Partners in Crime*, the theatre was robbed, so Ivan dragged out the safe and displayed it on the sidewalk in front of the theatre with a sign saying: "See What *Partners in Crime* did to us." Theatre circuit bigwigs were not impressed but business boomed. When neon signs came in, the Dominion's stained glass ceiling was lit from below by a series of neon tubes, the largest neon ceiling in Canada.

Ivan left the Dominion and became manager of the Capitol Theatre in Victoria where he promoted the first all-talking motion picture made in Canada, *The Crimson Paradise*, produced and filmed in Victoria by Commonwealth Productions Limited. It was first screened Thursday, December 14, 1933 at 11:00 p.m. Ackery says of *The Crimson Paradise*, "this turkey was financed by a wealthy family for the glorification of same. It kept the house full for two weeks just before Christmas with a curiosity crowd; it never played to a full house again." In the early thirties he became manager of the great

The long elaborate lobby of Thomas Lamb's Vancouver Capitol was quite similar to his Pantages in Toronto. Ivan Ackery began his career here as a singing usher.

A young Cary Grant with Ivan Ackery,
manager of the Vancouver Orpheum.

Orpheum Theatre and worked his magic there. Ivan Ackery's Orpheum usherettes became very well-known. Among them were Juliette of CBC fame and Yvonne De Carlo, who got her big break while dancing on the Orpheum stage.

Many well-known Hollywood stars made personal appearances at the Orpheum. Frank Sinatra appeared there in 1933 with the "Hoboken Kids."

Several stars became personal friends of Ackery. They could be lured away from Hollywood to the relative quiet of Vancouver to escape the rat race, perhaps to take a trip to the interior for fishing or sightseeing or even to spend a week at Ivan Ackery's beautiful home overlooking the ocean. Gary Cooper and George Burns were just two of the stars who did that. (There is a marvellous picture which George Burns has given to Ivan with the inscription "Dear Ivan—I'd love to forget you". It always brings a good laugh from Ivan whenever he looks at it.) Jack Benny met Mary Livingstone backstage at the old Orpheum theatre and that's where their romance began. Benny was paid $150 per week at the old Orpheum. Mark Kenny's famous Canadian band started there and several world premieres were held, one of them under the patronage of Princess Margaret.

Show business publicist and lifelong friend, Theo Ross of Vancouver had a hard time keeping up with Ackery's list of

Hollywood stars and personalities. Sometimes Ivan's efforts to keep things in the showbiz tradition backfired. On one memorable occasion, Ivan's dog got into the act. Ivan would often carry his little white poodle onto the stage where it would trot along beside him and Susan Hayward, or whoever happened to be the featured

The Vogue Theatre, Vancouver, B.C. was designed by Sprachman and Kaplan in a charming Art Deco style.

star. The dog always looked extremely small on that giant stage and this gave the impression that the theatre was even bigger. One day the dog marched across the stage in his usual fashion but stopped abruptly and piddled right into the hidden stage microphone! The house literally broke up with hysterical gales of laughter because it really sounded as if the Boulder Dam had just burst into the orchestra pit! One of Ackery's more successful publicity stunts occurred when he disrupted Vancouver traffic with 130 milk wagons and horses as he tried to find Vancouver's most handsome milkman in order to plug the movie, *The Kid from Brooklyn*, which was about a milkman, starring Danny Kaye. Show business magazines equate Ackery in Canada with "Roxy" in the United States.

One of the smaller American movie theatre circuits was owned by Warner Bros. Theatres bearing the name "Warners" later became casualties of the American Anti-Combines Act which forced studios to divest themselves of their theatre properties. The first Warner Brothers theatre owned by Sam, Jack and Albert Warner, opened in the town of New York, Pennsylvania, in 1906. (When he was very young, Jack Warner had lived in Canada.) Warner Brothers built theatres in many of America's larger cities but none in Canada. Perhaps the most famous was The Warner Western (later the Wiltern) in Los Angeles which saw many grand Hollywood premieres. It was designed in Art Deco, featuring "Zigzag Moderne" treatments done in tones of soft green and shades of gold. The architect was Albert Landsburg. It was supposed to show only Warner Brothers pictures, of course, just as William Fox's theatres showed only Paramount pictures and, considerably later, 20th Century Fox pictures. After the Anti-Combines Act, this all changed, and by 1932, the Warner Western had closed. It remained closed for some time but was later magnificently restored by developer Wayne Ratkovich in the mid-1980s.

The gigantic Fox Theatre in Detroit, of the great Fox Circuit, is the second largest theatre in America. It is still unquestionably one of the most spectacular movie palaces anywhere in the world. It was the favourite theatre of Canada's famous O'Connor Sisters, who played all the great theatres in North America. "Oh the fabulous Fox, what a wonderful place! We played there

This brochure used by a theatre supplier showed theatre owners the removable letters available for purchase.

for 22 weeks straight!" Vera O'Connor says. The O'Connor sisters played the Fox as a trio in 1929. Even though the Fox programme advertised 6,000 seats, the trio of Kathleen, Mary and Madeline had the microphones shut off and still filled the place with sound. "We never had any trouble being heard over the wonderful sixty-five piece theatre orchestra either," Madeline O'Connor says. "These so-called superstar singers today couldn't be heard in the second row! We were trained to project our voices in the great vaudeville theatres like the Majestic in Chicago. It took a lot of practice but we could be heard in the biggest of theatres." Six voices, or even three for that matter, are louder than one, but still there were very few singers with powerful voices like that. "Kate Smith was a great singer. She had all the volume you could ask for too," Vera says,

Detroit's "Fabulous Fox" theatre. The staggering seating capacity (advertised at 6,000) makes it one of the largest movie palaces in the world.

> *Of all the stars we knew, we loved Gracie Allen (they knew her before she selected George Burns to star with her) and Jimmy Durante the best. Whenever we went to see a show ourselves, we never, ever had to pay for a ticket, we were always the guest of the theatre's management. Sometimes when we sat in the boxes of a theatre, the actors would bow to us and acknowledge us from the stage, as would the orchestra conductors. It was a wonderful life really, but then not long after 1929 it all went downhill fast.*

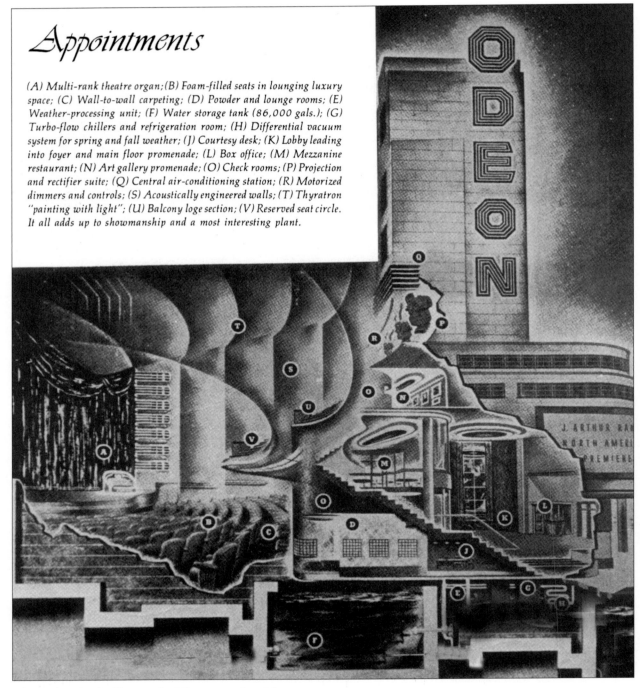

Appointments

(A) Multi-rank theatre organ; (B) Foam-filled seats in lounging luxury space; (C) Wall-to-wall carpeting; (D) Powder and lounge rooms; (E) Weather-processing unit; (F) Water storage tank (86,000 gals.); (G) Turbo-flow chillers and refrigeration room; (H) Differential vacuum system for spring and fall weather; (J) Courtesy desk; (K) Lobby leading into foyer and main floor promenade; (L) Box office; (M) Mezzanine restaurant; (N) Art gallery promenade; (O) Check rooms; (P) Projection and rectifier suite; (Q) Central air-conditioning station; (R) Motorized dimmers and controls; (S) Acoustically engineered walls; (T) Thyratron "painting with light"; (U) Balcony loge section; (V) Reserved seat circle. It all adds up to showmanship and a most interesting plant.

This brochure for the Odeon was handed out on opening night.

(So fast in fact, that the O'Connor Sisters were running a little restaurant at The Canadian National Exhibition a season or so later.)

The Americans were not the only ones who were looking at Canada as a future market for theatre holdings; there were also the British. The huge British Odeon theatre circuit made inroads into Canada after the Second World War but could not penetrate the United States market. In 1978, Odeon Theatres of Canada Limited was sold to an all-Canadian company, Canadian Odeon. With its 250 screens in 168 theatres, it was the largest, wholly Canadian-owned theatre

Not all of Canada's smaller movie theatre circuits were gobbled up by the aggressive Famous Players circuit. Some, like the O'Briens of northern Ontario, managed to survive.

circuit in Canada. Later it was to become the backbone of Cineplex-Odeon before the company became one of America's largest movie theatre chains. Until 1999, Cineplex-Odeon had its headquarters on Yonge St. in Toronto. Because of driving force, Garth Drabinsky, Canadian-operated movie theatres were on the world map once again.

In order to survive, independent theatres and small theatre circuits all over North America have had to buck the huge distribution companies and the circuits. It is a very competitive business in which only the strong survive. What is amazing is that some independent theatres are still operating in America.

The movie industry has survived many upheavals. The first was the introduction of sound to movies. Even the big circuits

Portrait in Black, (1960). *In the 60s and 70s, many grand movie palaces were divided into small theatres.*

nearly collapsed when sound came in. The popularity of radio was another crisis. When the Depression hit, movies suffered along with every other business. Television was perhaps the most serious threat and when it became popular, theatres saw attendance drop by the millions.

There were very few movie palaces built after 1929 because of the Depression and the introduction of sound movies. Who could afford to build? The Rockefeller family built Radio City Music Hall in New York City in 1932, but for other, more ordinary mortals, money was hard to borrow and the construction industry was in bad shape. Many movie studios in the United States were also in trouble financially. Sound might have been poor but it was new and it offered something the silent picture could not. American trade magazines at the time reported that the nearly 5,000 theatres that closed were simply sold and reopened again by somebody else. However, the situation reflected the uncertainty which spread throughout the industry.

MGM had its last big moneymakers, like Rock Hudson and Doris Day's *Pillow Talk*, in the 1960s, and soon after it went out of business as a big production company. The old Hollywood "star factories" were gone forever and MGM's problems were shared by all its competitors. A few still produce some films but they are more than likely owned by other, more diversified companies. Hollywood is not the same. The multi-corporate company is now in the driver's seat with firms like Gulf and Western owning Paramount Pictures. Even the big movie back lots are disappearing.

Hollywood studios have had to change and so have the theatres which show their movies. Unfortunately for the movie patron and the movie palaces, the changes have not always been for the best. Perhaps the most significant changes have taken place in the distribution of movies and the flight of the movie-going public to the suburbs.

Movie companies now demand enormous percentages of box office receipts. In some theatres, blockbuster movies like *E.T., Return of the Jedi, Star Wars, Titanic, Star Wars, Episode I: The Phantom Menace,* return to their makers 80 percent or more of box office receipts, after the "house nut" or theatre operating expenses have been covered in the first month. The longer the picture runs, the greater the percentage of receipts the theatre can keep. Therefore the pressure is always on a movie theatre to keep a picture for a long time. George Lucas' *Return of the Jedi* made an incredible six million dollars on the first day! More

Montreal's Outremont Theatre opened in 1929, one of the few ornate neighbourhood theatres.

The Outremont featured side walls in the atmospheric tradition with a proscenium arch festooned with bas-relief dancing figures.

recent films have made even more money, but such movies are a rarity.

To ensure an audience for a month or longer, theatre owners began to build smaller theatres. Smaller, multi-screen theatres also solved another dilemma for the theatre owner. In order to get the blockbuster movie, owners are often forced to contract for a weak movie as well. By having a multi-screen cinema, weak films could be buried in the smallest cinema, while Cinema 1 showed the big picture.

The deterioration of big city cores in the United States in the 1960s and 1970s also encouraged theatre owners to build their cinemas in the suburbs where their audiences were. In many cities, people were too frightened to come downtown to see a movie. This was not the case in Canada, but new cinemas were built in the suburban malls for financial reasons. It seemed the movie palace was doomed. The lovely Fox Detroit, with its more than 5,000 seats, could not afford to contract for the weak movies, nor could it afford to rent a good movie when some distribution companies based the rental price of the film on the number of seats in the house. The Fox survived by replacing its movies with rock concerts and other forms of live entertainment. The "Fabulous Foxes" in both Detroit and St. Louis are looking better than ever and will still be impressing audiences well into the millennium. A few facts about the famous Detroit theatre: the enormous auditorium is 200 feet long, 175 feet wide, and 110 feet high. The balcony is the largest clear-span in the world (no pillars hold it up). The chandelier in the auditorium ceiling is 13 feet in diameter, weighs two tons, contains more than 1,200 pieces of leaded glass and holds 210 light bulbs. The staff originally numbered over 400. The Fox orchestra was made up of 60 musicians, the choir numbered 50 and the "Fox Tillerettes" (chorus line) had 32 high steppers.

It is not surprising that restoring the Detroit Fox cost a great deal and required the hard work and dedication of many people. In 1981, Robert Werbe began with a $2 million renovation. This was followed by Charles Forbes and "Friends of the Fox" in 1987, and was climaxed when Mike Ilith bought the place and pumped another $8 million into a complete renovation. The Motown Record Company sponsored reviews and rock concerts which helped to make the Fox a moneymaker.

The Detroit Fox features an enormous balcony with no pillars making it the largest clear-span balcony in the world.

The Imperial Theatre, Montreal (1913) is a fine example of an early legitimate theatre. It later converted to movies and for years it showed first-run Hollywood blockbusters. Its livery of red and gold looks good even today.

Even the great Radio City Music Hall in New York ran into difficulty with its policy of presenting both a hit movie and a stage show. By the end of the 1970s, a crisis point had arrived. The end seemed very near when the great Radio City Music Hall was scheduled to close its doors in March 1979. It is ironic that as a result of a television special starring Ann-Margret, Greer Garson and Gregory Peck done the previous year to draw attention to its plight, the theatre was given a $2.5 million shot in the arm and was declared a "landmark for the State of New York." It now features spectacular stage shows and special entertainment productions and is able to sell tickets months in advance.

Many great movie theatres have been converted to civic centres or to concert halls. Others are being converted into twin-screen or multi-screen theatres. This twinning process is not always disastrous from an architectural point of view because the twinning can be reversed. The average twinning process usually means that a floor is built from the first row of the balcony to some point just above the downstairs movie screen, which has been essentially cut in half. Theatres can be twinned in two weeks and untwinned in less time than that. For them there is still hope.

The main concessions stand of Famous Players' Toronto Colossus theatre. The Colossus features 18 stadium-seating auditoriums, THX sound, an IMAX screen with 3D capacity and "the Pod," a fully licensed lounge.

Designed to resemble a giant UFO landing site, the design of Famous Players Colossus is meant to attract a younger audience.

The Imperial Theatre in Montreal, although once split, has been restored to its original stunning condition by its owners, United Cinemas of Quebec (which is in turn owned by Famous Players). Although no longer a movie house, it is still very much alive. In many cases, the buildings that undergo twinning are not architecturally damaged and the final result is relatively attractive. Such was the case of the Runnymede in Toronto. For some theatres however, the renovation has been disastrous, like in the case of the old Pantages theatre, later the Imperial Six, in Toronto. Thankfully, Garth Drabinsky restored it beautifully by gutting the place and virtually starting again. The Pantages name was also restored.

Many Canadians have left their mark in theatre and movie history. In 1896, Ottawa's Holland Brothers presented Edison's Vitascope at Koster and Bial's Music Hall and made movies part of a theatrical performance for the first time in North America. Film star Mary Pickford reigned Queen of the silent-movie era and helped revolutionize the movie-making industry by co-founding United Artists in 1919. In the 1910s, Queen's University Professor Herbert Kalmus took his invention "Colour by Technicolor" to Hollywood and changed the look of movies forever.

Canadians also founded the first international theatre circuit—the Allen Circuit—which spread from its humble beginnings in Brantford, Ontario across the country and into the United States. In more recent times, the Canadian-owned Cineplex Odeon became an international giant by pioneering the multi-plexed auditorium concept. But perhaps most impressive, Canadians built and operated some of the world's largest and most beautiful pre-1920 vaudeville theatres— magical places that mixed old world elegance with the excitement and energy of a circus. The most famous, Toronto's Shea's Hippodrome, could transport audiences away to a different time and place, which was what going to the theatre was all about.

While the days of the classic movie palace seem gone for good, live theatre has undergone a spirited renaissance in recent years. As a result, grand opera houses and vaudeville theatres are being restored across the country to host a booming theatre industry. Furthermore, public and private preservation societies such as Historic Theatres' Trust (H.T.T.) are well-organized and devoted to saving Canada's threatened theatres from the wrecking ball. Under the dynamic leadership of Janet MacKinnon,

H.T.T. has documented vanishing pieces of theatre history necessary for theatre preservation and renovation. Similar societies operate in the United States (The Theatre Historical Society of America and The League of Historic Theatres), as well as in Britain and Australia. In addition, all of these organizations cooperate with various theatre organ societies. The efforts of these groups often go unnoticed, but the national treasures they have saved are there for everyone to enjoy.

Theatre restoration expert, David Hannivan, is responsible for restoring the painting and gilt in the Elgin and Winter Garden, as well as in theatres across North America.

Autumn in the Winter Garden

Acknowledgements

Palaces of the Night could not have been produced without the assistance of many people and organizations. The author would like to thank the staff at Lynx Images Inc. for their dedication to this project. In particular, Russell Floren for spearheading its production, Andrea Gutsche for her brilliant book design and for her superb photographic memory, Barbara Chisholm for her care and proficiency in revising the text, Steve Gamester for his co-ordinating dexterity, Jennifer Hart for her marketing skills and Katharine Knowles and Janice Carter for assisting with graphics. Thanks also to Deborah Wise Harris for her excellent copy editing.

Special thanks to the following:

My wife Patricia and daughter Rebecca for assistance in the preparation of the manuscript, my daughter Jennifer for her patience and understanding, and Paul Forsyth, chief project photographer, for the use of his private theatre archives.

Additional thanks to Brother Andrew Corsini and Terry Helgessen (The Theatre Historical Society of America), Chris Darling, Patrick Dooley, Allan Dudeck, Tom Einhouse and Ruth Flannery (Playhouse Square Centre, Cleveland, Ohio), Larry Fischer, Izz Gang and Bernie Venus (Toronto Theatre Organ Society), Peter and Marie Graham, David Hannivan, Roma Hewitt, Doreen Leger, Dane Lanken, Gerald Lenton, Robert Leslie, Barrett Lindsay-Kolari, Scott Lindsay, Janet MacKinnon (Historic Theatres Trust), The Mary Pickford Company, Steve Rabbetts, David Renegar, Mandel Sprachman.

Grateful assistance was received from Lin Bennett, Stanley Theatre, Vancouver, B.C.; Karen Brandt and Dudley Dumond, Famous Players Theatres; Suzanne Deitrich, Empress Theatre, Fort Macleod, Alberta; Patrick Dooley and Helena Aalto, Runnymede Theatre, Toronto, Ont.; Chris Doty and Shelia Johnston, Grand Theatre, London, Ont.; Bonnie Ellis, Vogue Theatre, Vancouver, B.C.; Michael Grit, Sanderson Centre for the Performing Arts, Brantford, Ont.; Patti and David Hannivan, Hannivan and Co.; Sylvie Jacques, Le Capitole de Québec, Québec; Donna King, Orpheum Theatre, Vancouver, B. C.; Arnie Lappin, Elgin and Winter Garden Theatre Centre, Toronto, Ont.; Christine Manore, Capitol Theatre, Moncton, N.B.; Uwe Meyer and Michael Wallace, Capitol Theatre, Port Hope, Ont.; David and Ed Mirvish and Robert Brockhouse, The Royal Alexandra Theatre, Toronto, Ont.; Rick Ostapchuk, Princess, Garneau, and Roxy Theatres, Edmonton, Alta.; François Poisson, Salle J.A. Thomson (Capitol Theatre), Trois-Rivières, Que.; Kim Prangley, Haskell Opera House, Rock Island, Que.; Miriam Shostak and Kerry Swartz, McPhearson Playhouse and Royal Theatres, Victoria, B.C.; Richard Sklenar, Playhouse Square, Cleveland, Ohio; Peter Smith, Imperial Theatre, Saint John, N.B.

Picture Credits

Allen Theatre, Playhouse Square, Cleveland. Photographer: David Thum: 129, 182; Bruce Young Col'n 181
Gary Beechey, bds studios: x,222
Roy Bingham Collection, Melborne, England: 98.155.161-161
Capitol Theatre, Moncton: 63 t.,122 b.,126 b.r.,188
Capitol Theatre, Montreal. Photographer: Brian Merrett: 100
Capitol Theatre, Port Hope. Photographer: Michael Wallace, Imagelink Studio, Port Hope: 99,117b.
Le Capitole de Québec, Québec: 123,124
Bill Cousintine Collection, Hunstville, Ontario: 13,19,116,137,151,168,176,189
Chris Darling Collection, Hollywood California: 2,3-4,13,14,15 t.,40,42 t.,49,51,55,66 t.,103,112,114,115,116,148-149,151,
    176,178,189,191 t.,194,214
Elgin and Winter Garden Theatre Centre, Toronto: 73-80,82,83,223,120,121t.,126 b.l.,127 t.l.
Famous Players Theatres: 30,46,47,48 b.,52,57,58,59,60 b.,62 m.,62 b.,64,70-71,84,86-87,104,131,144,186,19
(Photographer: Richard Johnson); Photographer: Tom Sandler: 219-220
Paul Forsyth Photography Collection, Toronto: 31-32,38,43,64,70 b.,89,117t.,130b.,142,151,154,159,162,164,165,168,
    183,211,217,218
Geraldine, Madeline, and Vera O'Connor Collection, Port Credit, Ontario: 36-37,39
Glenbow Institute, Calgary: 8,10,11,12,16 t.,20,21,55,103,177,179
Grand Theatre, London, Ontario: 24,25,29,172
David Hannivan Collection, Toronto: 27 1.,132b.,191,192,223
Haskell Opera House, Rock Island, Quebec. Photographer: Don Whipple, Whipple's Studio: 125
Historic Theatres' Trust, Emmanuel Briffa Collection, Montreal: 15,17,61 m.r.,61 b.r.,61 m.l.,65-66 b.,67-68,118,172, 174,
    175,179,184-185,187,202,204
Imperial Oil Review 121b.
Imperial Theatre, Saint John: 27,122 t.,132 b.
Dane Lanken: 63 m.,63 b.
John Lindsay Collection, Toronto, Ont.: iv,13,22-23,27,35,36,42,45,48,50,53,57-58,60 t.,62 t.l.,69 t.,94,96,97,102,109,105-
    106,110,113,121 b.,128,135,137,140,141,144-147,150,213,171,173,176 b.,179,186,190,191b.,199,205-208,210
The Mary Pickford Company, Hollywood, California: forward,42 b.,50
Metropolitan Toronto Reference Library—Theatre Department, Toronto: 6,19,26,29,30,34,48 t.,52,71,143
Odeon Theatres of Canada: 22 t.,193,212
Orpheum Theatre, Vancouver Civic Theatres, Vancouver. Photographer: David Blue: 130 t.,188,203
Parks Canada: 1-2,4-5,6-7,127 t.p.,133-134
Provincial Archives of Nova Scotia, Halifax: 26 b.,28
Royal Theatre and McPhearson Playhouse, Victoria. Photographer: Kerry Swartz: 18,44,131b.,188
Sanderson Centre for the Performing Arts, Brantford. Photographer: Anthony Stocco: 127 b.,132 t.
Fiona Spalding-Smith: 126 t.,139
Stanley Theatre, Vancouver. Photographer: Anthony Fulker: 196,197
Théâtre Outremont, Montreal: 215-216
Don Thompson Collection, Aurora, Ontario: 155,161,164,167
Salle J. A. Thomson (Capitol Theatre), Trois-Rivières: 152-153
Toronto Theatre Organ Society: 35,156,157,158,163,168
Brooke Townsend, Toronto: 47,213
United Theatres Inc., Quebec: 41,91,92-93
Vancouver Public Library: 195
Vogue Theatre, Vancouver: 209
Ken Young Photography, Toronto: 81,200-201

About the Author

John C. Lindsay, Toronto writer and freelance broadcaster, has been a lifelong movie lover. He has explored theatres in dozens of cities in many parts of the world, and has been fascinated by both the buildings themselves and by the life around them. Mr. Lindsay graduated from the University of Western Ontario and from the Faculty of Education of the University of Toronto. He has been a guest lecturer at several Canadian Universities and has appeared on many radio and television shows. His vast knowledge of theatres and theatrical lore have made him a leading authority on Canadian theatre history. *Palaces of the Night: Canada's Grand Theatres* is Lindsay's most comprehensive book on theatre.

About Lynx Images

Lynx Images is a unique book publishing and film production company that specializes in exploring and documenting vanishing pieces of Canadian history. The company's Canadian focus has generated several best-selling books and films:

- *Mysterious Islands: Forgotten Tales of the Great Lakes*
- *Northern Lights: Lighthouses of Canada*
- *Superior: Under the Shadow of the Gods*
- *Enchanted Summers: The Grand Hotels of Muskoka*
- *Ghosts of the Bay: The Forgotten History of Georgian Bay*
- *Alone in the Night: Lighthouses of Georgian Bay, Manitoulin Island and the North Channel*
- *The North Channel and St. Mary's River: A Guide to the History*

Index

(italicized page numbers indicate photographs)